T0035584

AMAZING SPACE

Written by Arwen Hubbard
Models designed and built by Simon Pickard and Tim Goddard

Contents

Arecibo message, p87

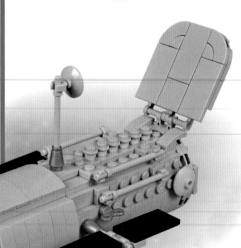

Comet, p54

Hubble Telescope, p70

Valles Marineris, p59

James Webb Space Telescope, p32

Arecibo radio telescope, p86

Dawn spacecraft,
p36

Our Place in Space

Welcome to the universe! We have only just begun to explore it. So far, we know it is a very, very big place, full of swirling galaxies, shining stars, mysterious black holes, and, of course, the little blue planet we call home—Earth. Let's take a look around and see what else there is to discover.

Where did everything come from?

Scientists think that 13.8 billion years ago, everything in our universe was squeezed together in a hot, dense state. Suddenly the universe started to expand in a moment known as the Big Bang. As the universe grew and cooled, atoms formed and became the building blocks of stars, planets, galaxies, and us.

COVER YOUR EARS—IT'S THE BIG BANG!

WOW!
Space is expanding **everywhere** at once. There is no center of the universe.

Did you know?

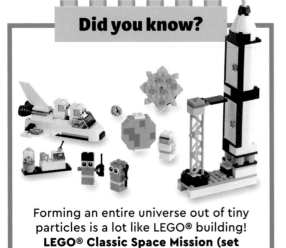

Forming an entire universe out of tiny particles is a lot like LEGO® building! **LEGO® Classic Space Mission (set 11022)** even has instructions for building simple planets and suns!

Getting bigger

The universe has continued to expand since the Big Bang. Scientists are working hard to learn more about the early universe and how it has changed over time. Recent observations of faraway galaxies show that the expansion of the universe is speeding up as it gets older and bigger.

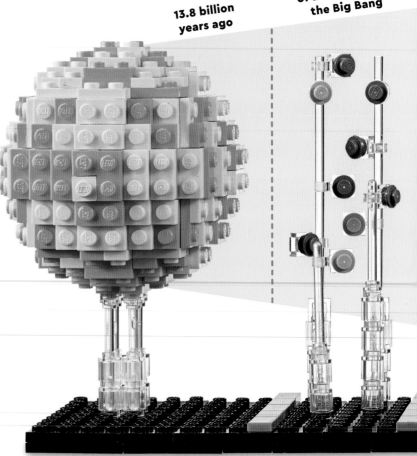

13.8 billion years ago

1 ten-thousandth of a second after the Big Bang

The Big Bang

The first matter appears

All aglow

In every direction we look in space, scientists find a glow left over from the Big Bang called the cosmic microwave background (CMB) radiation. Radiation is energy that moves in waves, like light. Studying this radiation can tell scientists about the early universe.

High speed

The speed of light is the limit as to how fast things inside the universe can move. The distance light can travel in one year is called a light-year. Light-years are used to measure how far apart things are in space. It takes time for light to travel, so the farther away we look, the further back in time we can study. Scientists can see almost as far back as the Big Bang!

REALLY!

One light-year is about **6 trillion miles** (10 trillion km)! The closest star you can see at night is about four light-years away. That is 24 trillion miles (39 trillion km).

BUILD IT!

These galaxies may be the biggest things you will ever make—using just 10 LEGO pieces! Use tooth or horn parts for the spiral arms and 1×1 plates with clips to hold everything together.

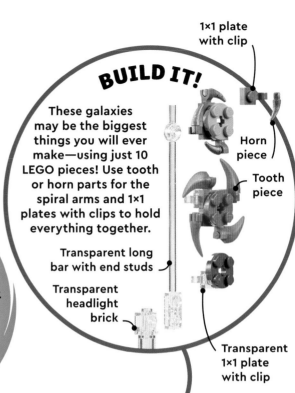

1×1 plate with clip

Horn piece

Tooth piece

Transparent long bar with end studs

Transparent headlight brick

Transparent 1×1 plate with clip

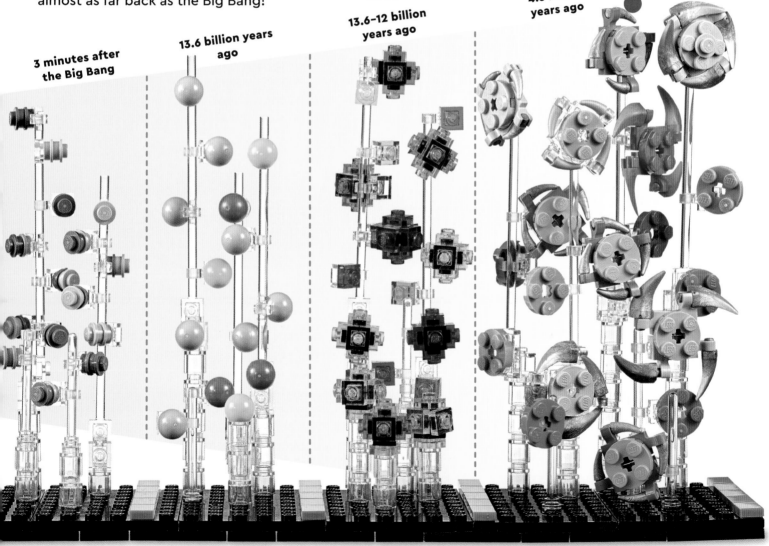

4.5 billion years ago

13.6–12 billion years ago

13.6 billion years ago

3 minutes after the Big Bang

Atoms form

The first stars start to shine

Galaxies begin to form

Modern galaxies—the solar system is born

What is space made of?

Space is full of amazing objects like stars, black holes, nebulae, planets, and asteroids. Even though there are lots of things in space, it is mostly empty because things are really far apart from each other. Everything in space is made from matter and energy. We think all the energy in the universe has existed since the Big Bang. Energy can't be created or destroyed—it just changes from one form to another.

WOW!

Scientists think that **5/6** of all matter in the universe is a mysterious invisible substance called **dark matter**, different from the familiar elements.

BUILD IT!

This friendly alien has horn pieces for their armlike tentacles—or are they tentaclelike arms? A white 1×2 plate makes the wide grin that stretches across their face!

Pointy head made from 1×1 slopes

Eyes are printed round tiles

"Arms" slot into 1×1 bricks with side studs

A comet has a blue gas tail and a white dust tail

This star's color shows it is not as hot as a blue star

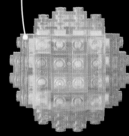

Mercury is the closest planet to the sun

Black holes occur when stars collapse

Matter and energy

Matter is the stuff that things are made from. Stars, planets, and people are made from a kind of matter called elements. Elements are like LEGO bricks; you can put them together in different ways to create new things! Energy is something stuff has when it is moving, or could be moving, like when a spring is pushed down ready to pop up.

Twinkle, twinkle

Stars are giant, glowing balls of hot plasma. Their centers are like nuclear furnaces making new elements. Stars smash together tiny pieces of elements called atoms to make even heavier atoms. These atoms become part of new stars and planets.

Blue supergiant stars are very young

Molecules of gas and dust exist in the space between the stars

Mars's rusty soil is the reason it's known as the Red Planet

WOW! I DON'T KNOW WHERE TO LOOK FIRST!

Earth is the only planet in our solar system where liquid water is found on the surface

Did you know?

LEGO sets with light and sound bricks convert electrical energy into waves of energy that you can see or hear. The light and sound is then absorbed into its surroundings as very small amounts of heat energy.

Space in space

Galaxies are huge collections of stars, gas, and dust held together by gravity. There is lots of empty space in galaxies between stars, but from far away, galaxies look like one big object.

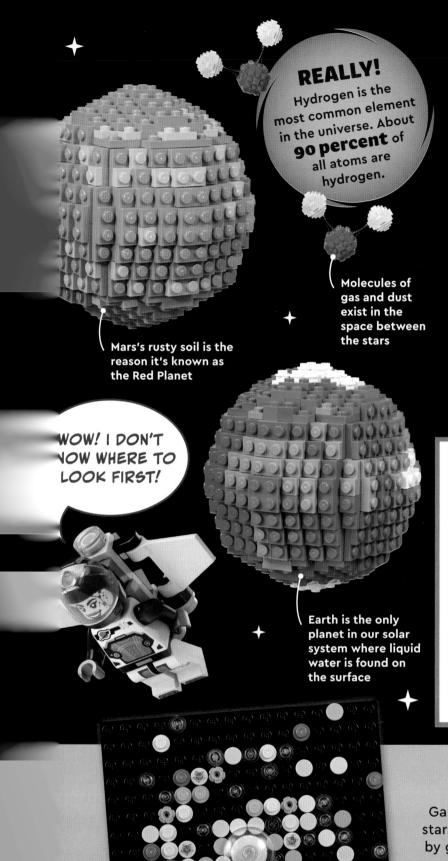

Small galaxies only contain a few million stars

How big is space?

We know that space is really, REALLY big. But scientists don't agree on how big the universe is yet. Some think that it is infinitely big—meaning it goes on forever! Others think that it must have a finite (or limited) size. What scientists do agree on is that there are hundreds of billions of galaxies, each with billions of stars in them.

WOW!

The Andromeda Galaxy is the farthest thing you can see with your own eyes. Its light takes more than **2 million** years to reach Earth!

BUILD IT!

This ship's impressive engine housing is made from two LEGO® Technic pieces threaded onto a LEGO Technic axle. One end of the axle plugs into a cross-hole brick at the back of the main hull.

LEGO Technic axle

LEGO Technic turbine wheel

LEGO Technic wheel

1×2 brick with cross hole

It takes a spacecraft just a few minutes to get into orbit

The sun vs. Earth

Stars, such as the sun, are enormous compared to planets. If the sun were the size of a beach ball, Earth would be about as big as a pea! Jupiter would be the size of a golf ball.

The sun

Earth

Star quality

The sun is a yellow dwarf star. This means it is a lot smaller than some stars, despite the fact that it is 864,000 miles (1,390,000 km) in diameter. Some stars are thousands of times the size of the sun!

The sun is mainly made of hydrogen

WOW! I'M STARSTRUCK!

The nearest any spacecraft has got to the sun is 4 million miles (6.4 million km)

REALLY!
Whenever you look at the night sky, you are looking **back in time**! It takes time for the stars' light to travel across space to your eyes.

Did you know?

One way to think about the size of space is in terms of LEGO minifigures! You would need to stack 9.5 billion astronaut minifigures to reach from Earth to the moon, and 9.5 trillion to get all the way to Mars!

Observable universe

We can only see objects within a bubble of space where light has had time to reach us since the birth of the universe about 13.8 billion years ago. We can't see what is beyond the observable universe, but space itself extends far beyond this boundary.

Where are we in space?

We live on a small planet called Earth, orbiting (going around) a small star called the sun, which is orbiting the center of a galaxy called the Milky Way. All the things that orbit around the sun are part of the solar system. As the sun travels through the Milky Way, it brings everything in the solar system along with it.

REALLY!
The solar system may be as big as two light-years across. It would take light **two years** to travel from one side to the other!

Comet

Asteroid belt

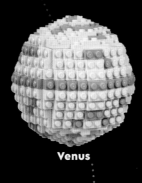
Venus

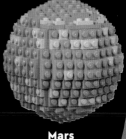

Earth

Mercury

Mars

WOW!
Many scientific words come from the ancient languages of Greek and Latin. **Sol** (as in "solar") means sun in Latin.

The sun

Solar system objects

The sun is in the middle of the solar system. There are lots of types of objects orbiting around it, ranging from giant gassy planets like Jupiter to chunks of rock and metal like asteroids and human-made spacecraft.

Earth's position

The solar system has different zones. Earth is in the inner solar system, which includes everything up to and including the asteroid belt. That means we are close to the sun, where it is hot. Earth's nearest neighbors are our moon, Mercury, Venus, and Mars.

Did you know?

The 450 pieces in **LEGO® Classic Creative Space Planets (set 11037)** can be used to make a whole model of the solar system or smaller space models, such as a glow-in-the-dark alien!

Saturn

Neptune

Kuiper belt

Jupiter

HANG A LEFT AT JUPITER!

Uranus

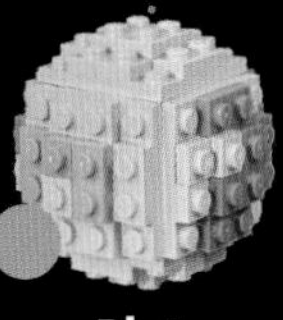

Pluto

BUILD IT!

To make a planet with studs on all sides, start with a core made from bricks with side studs. Use some of them upside down, as a mirror image of the ones above them. This method can be scaled up for all the planets shown here.

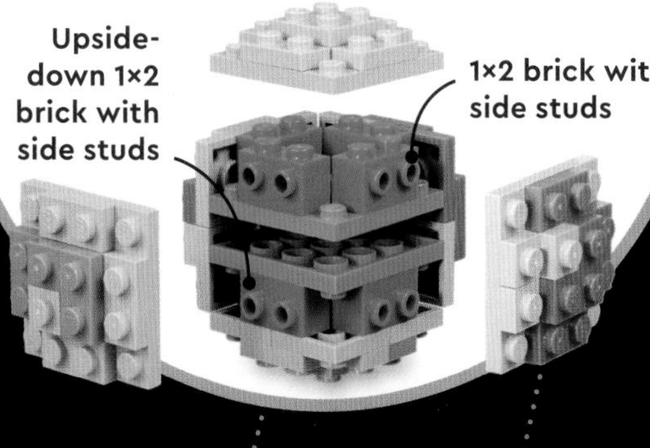

Upside-down 1×2 brick with side studs

1×2 brick with side studs

Galactic groups

Our galaxy is part of a vast group of galaxies called the Laniakea Supercluster. Laniakea is a Hawaiian word that means "immeasurable heavens." There are around 100,000 other galaxies in the supercluster.

Why is there life on Earth?

Earth has lots of things we don't find in space, such as liquid water to drink and air to breathe. Living beings like humans, other animals, and plants need food and habitats to survive. Earth's ecosystems provide those things. But Earth has not always been a good place for life. Earth has changed a lot over the past 4.5 billion years since it formed. It took millions of years for the ecosystems to grow.

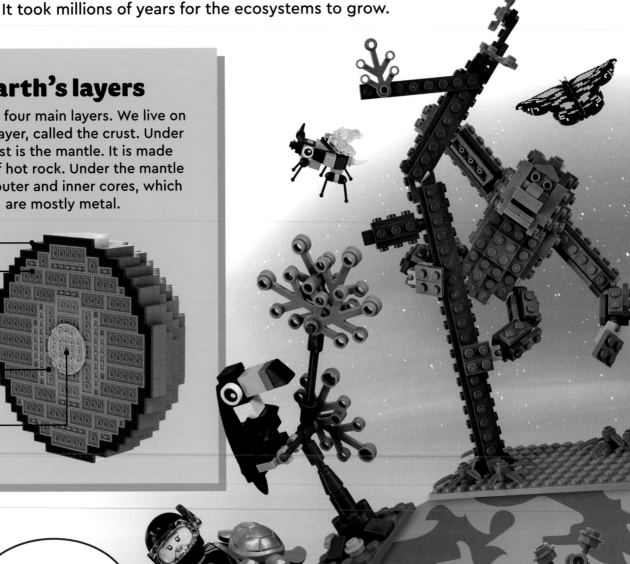

Earth's layers

Earth has four main layers. We live on the top layer, called the crust. Under the crust is the mantle. It is made mainly of hot rock. Under the mantle are the outer and inner cores, which are mostly metal.

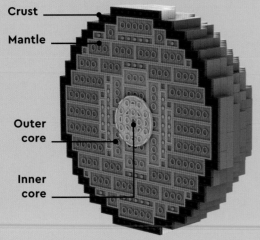

Crust

Mantle

Outer core

Inner core

EARTH IS TURTLEY AWESOME!

Water on Earth

When Earth first formed, it would have been too hot for liquid water. The oceans probably formed following millions of years of asteroids and comets smashing into the planet and delivering water from cooler regions of the solar system.

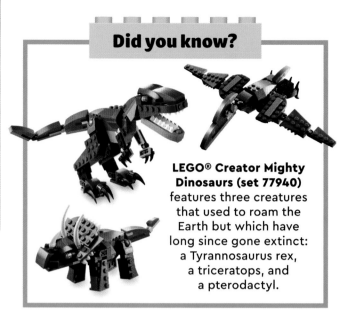

LEGO® Creator Mighty Dinosaurs (set 77940) features three creatures that used to roam the Earth but which have long since gone extinct: a Tyrannosaurus rex, a triceratops, and a pterodactyl.

REALLY!

Some of Earth's water may have been released into the air by **volcanoes**.

Magnetic field

Earth's outer core generates a giant magnetic field that surrounds the planet and protects it. This magnetic field is sometimes called the magnetosphere. It helps keep plants and animals safe from space radiation.

WOW!

Earth probably formed from lots of smaller pieces of **rock** and **metal** that were pulled together by gravity.

BUILD IT!

Put together this penguin's head by building out from a 1×1 brick with side studs all the way around. A sideways curved slope makes the smooth back of the head.

1×2 curved slope

1×1 brick with four side studs

Sideways 1×2 curved slope

Tooth piece

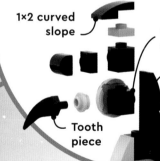

Why does the moon change shape?

WOW!
The moon **spins**, too! It spins at the same rate it goes around Earth, so we only ever see one side of it.

The moon orbits Earth. We can see the moon because light from the sun bounces off it. The sun can only light up the side of the moon that faces it, so one side is always lit, and the other is dark. As the moon goes around us, we can see different amounts of its lit side, which makes it appear as if the moon changes shape. These are the phases of the moon.

Waning crescent

REALLY!
Every year the moon **moves** a tiny bit farther away from Earth. It is moving away at about the same rate as your fingernails grow.

Last quarter

Waning gibbous

Total solar eclipse

Eclipses

Sometimes the moon gets between the sun and Earth and blocks the sun's light. This is called a solar eclipse, and can make daytime look like night. When Earth blocks sunlight from getting to the moon, it is called a lunar eclipse.

Journey time

The moon is about 238,900 miles (384,00 km) away from Earth. If you could drive there in a car at 60 mph (97 kph), it would take you about 166 days! The Apollo astronauts were going so fast that it only took them three days.

New moon

Waxing crescent

Making the moon

Scientists think the moon formed when a planet called Theia smashed into Earth 4.5 billion years ago. The collision sent big pieces of rock and metal into space that came together to form the moon.

First quarter

BUILD IT!

This model is built in the same way as the planets on page 17. Making it all gray and using 1×1 round plates with holes to represent craters is what makes it a realistic moon!

1×1 round plate with hole

MY FAVORITE PHASE IS THE WANING CRESCENT.

Waxing gibbous

Did you know?

In **LEGO® Ideas Tales of the Space Age (set 21340)**, round black elements are built onto gray ones to make a pair of crescent moons. They hang above a Martian landscape, complete with a microscale rover!

Full moon

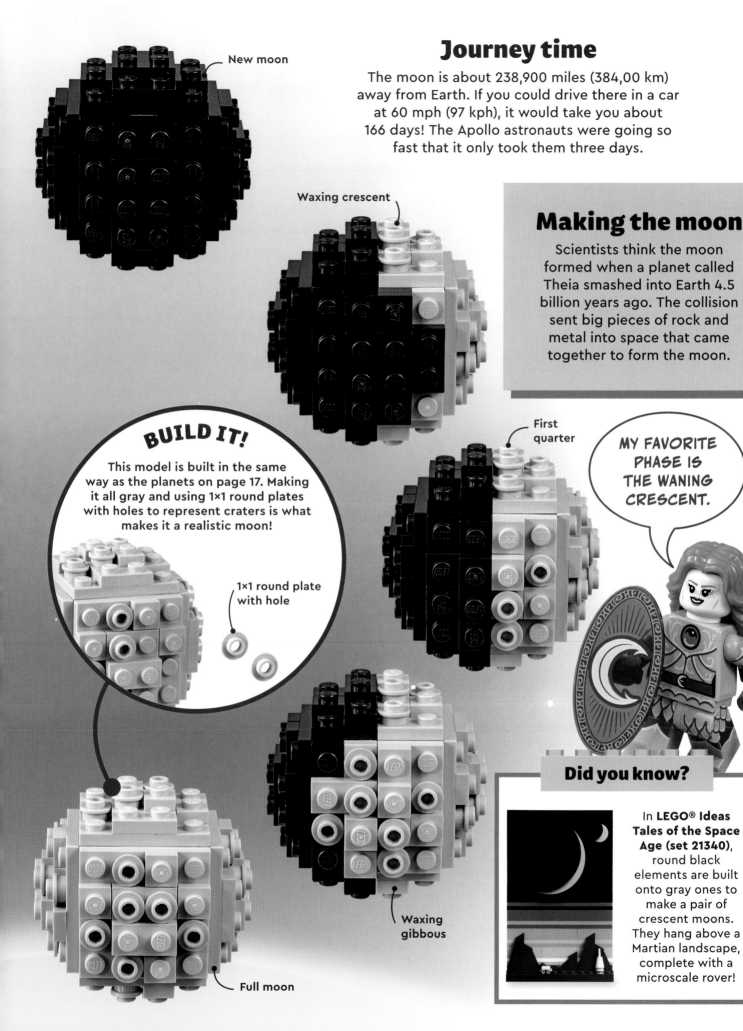

What's the moon made of?

The moon is made of rock and metal, just like Earth. It has a mantle, a crust, and a small core. But unlike Earth, the moon has almost no air. This means the side of the moon facing the sun gets very hot, and the side facing away gets very cold.

YEAH. DEFINITELY NOT MADE OF CHEESE!

Craters are caused by meteorites smashing into the moon's surface

Taking a walk

As long as you have a protective space suit, you can walk on the moon. It's a bouncy walk though, because the moon has just one-sixth of the gravity to pull you back to the surface! When you look up from the moon you can see the stars, but instead of the moon, you will see Earth in the sky!

REALLY!
The dark spots you see on the moon are actually made from **cooled lava.**

Leaving a mark

There is not enough air on the moon for wind or weather of any kind. So all the footprints and rover tracks left behind by astronauts who visited the moon in the 1960s and 1970s are still there!

Astronauts have placed flags on the moon

WOW!
The **far side** of the moon faces away from the Earth. It doesn't have as many dark spots as the side that faces Earth, and scientists aren't sure why!

Did you know?

The moon is not made of cake, but in LEGO® Monkie Kid™, it's where moon cakes are made! **LEGO Monkie Kid Chang'e Moon Cake Factory (set 80032)** even comes with a carrot-shaped rocket for sending the cakes back to Earth!

BUILD IT!

The sides of this crater are made from four curved round corner bricks. The rest of the lunar surface is built from slope bricks and wedge plates for a rough and rocky look.

3×3 curved round corner brick

TIME FOR AN ICY DIP.

Water on the moon

Planetary scientists have discovered frozen water on the moon! Water ice can exist where it is protected from sunlight underneath the moon's surface and in the bottoms of deep craters, where it is always shady.

How We Study Space

Every journey must begin somewhere. Humans have been studying space for as long as we have been able to look up and wonder about those strange points of light in the sky. We have told stories, used stars to find our way across vast oceans, and recorded the events of the night sky. Today, we have telescopes to peer even farther away and rockets to send rovers to distant worlds. What will we find next?

Who were the **first** space explorers?

Humans all over the world have looked up and wondered about the stars and planets. Early scientists tracked and recorded the positions of objects they saw in the night sky. Using observation, math, and logic, they learned a lot about the universe, even without the tools we have today. Some ancient monuments, like Stonehenge, may have been used to help people keep track of the night sky.

The 30 large stones may have represented 30 days in a month

WOW!

In 1054 CE, Chinese astronomers recorded the appearance of a **"guest star."** It was one of the only visible supernovas (explosions of stars) in recorded history.

BUILD IT!

Make realistic standing stones by building out from a stack of bricks with side studs. Then add rocky detailing on all sides, with only a few smooth sections.

1×1 brick with four side studs

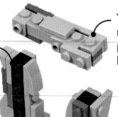

Top piece is made from plates and brackets

Ancient civilizations

Many civilizations around the globe based their calendars on the phases of the moon, the positions of stars, and the movements of planets. They paid attention to how objects in the sky moved night after night and year after year and predicted what they would do in the future.

The stones align with sunrise on the longest day and sunset on the shortest day of the year

REALLY!
A Greek mathematician named Eratosthenes calculated how big Earth was in the **3rd century** BCE. That was more than 2,000 years ago!

Around and around

Humans have had many ideas about the structure of the universe. In the 16th century, Polish astronomer Nicolaus Copernicus used math to show that the sun sits at the center of our solar system and that Earth is a planet moving around it.

Cotton sails

All at sea

Early seafarers were able to make long journeys navigating by the stars. From the 18th century, sailors at sea could use the positions of stars and the sun and a little bit of math to figure out where they were.

I NEED TO TAKE THIS SHOT BEFORE SUNSET.

Is there a map of the stars?

Humans have made many maps of the stars. One way we keep track of them is to divide the whole sky into constellations. Constellations are groups of stars. Sometimes these groups look like they make a picture. These pictures might look like creatures from mythology or objects in everyday life.

REALLY!
Stories about some constellations were passed down for thousands of years from the ancient **Mesopotamian** civilizations.

BUILD IT!

Short bar with stopper

1×1 jewel

1×1 tile with clip

1×2 jumper plate

Make the lines connecting this constellation using bars attached to tiles with clips. Use jumper plates wherever you need to position a star in between two studs.

The Little Dipper looks like a small pan or ladle

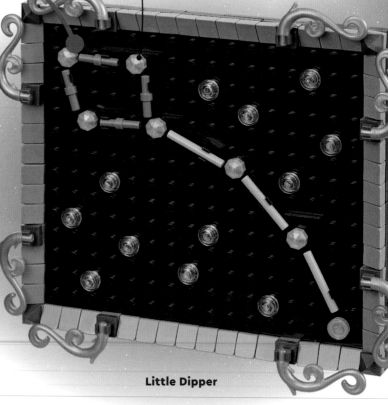

Little Dipper

Did you know?

LEGO® Friends Stargazing Camping Vehicle (set 42603) includes a brick-built night sky backdrop. You can rearrange its glow-in-the-dark stars to make different constellations for Nova and Aliya to spot!

Modern constellations

Today, 88 constellations are recognized by the International Astronomical Union (IAU). The IAU voted on which ones to include on their maps in 1928. The Big Dipper and Little Dipper are now just parts of the Great and Little Bear constellations.

Orion

Orion is one of the most recognizable constellations. If you connect the stars of Orion, they form the shape of what many people think looks like a giant hunter in the sky. Orion can be seen from anywhere in the world. It is most noticeable during the Northern Hemisphere's winter.

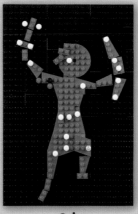

Orion

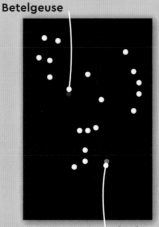

Betelgeuse

Rigel

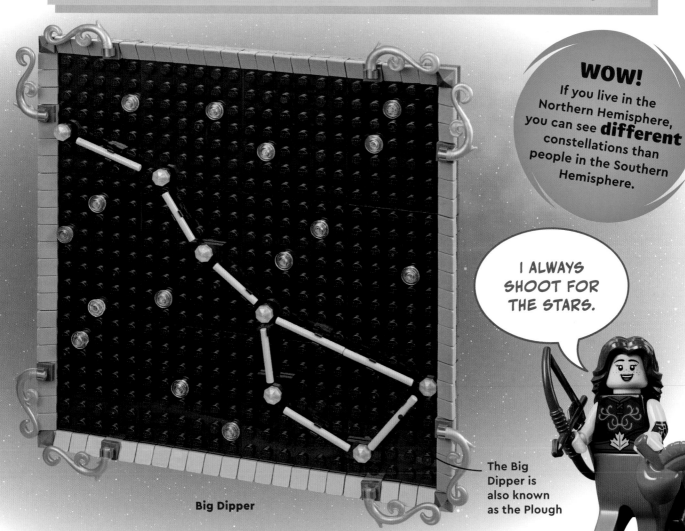

Big Dipper

WOW!
If you live in the Northern Hemisphere, you can see **different** constellations than people in the Southern Hemisphere.

I ALWAYS SHOOT FOR THE STARS.

The Big Dipper is also known as the Plough

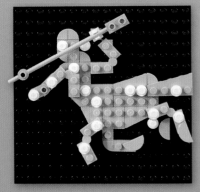

Centaurus

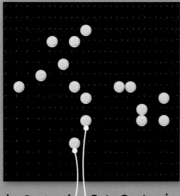

Alpha Centauri Beta Centauri

Naming stars

Some bright stars have proper names like Sirius, Betelgeuse, or Deneb, but others have a string of letters and numbers or are named after the constellation they are in. For example, Alpha Centauri is the brightest star in the constellation Centaurus. Beta Centauri is the second brightest.

How can we see space up close?

We can use telescopes to help us see things that are far away. Telescopes collect light. The bigger the telescope is, the more light it can collect and the more information we can get. Even though some places are too far away for us to reach with our spacecraft, we can study them from Earth.

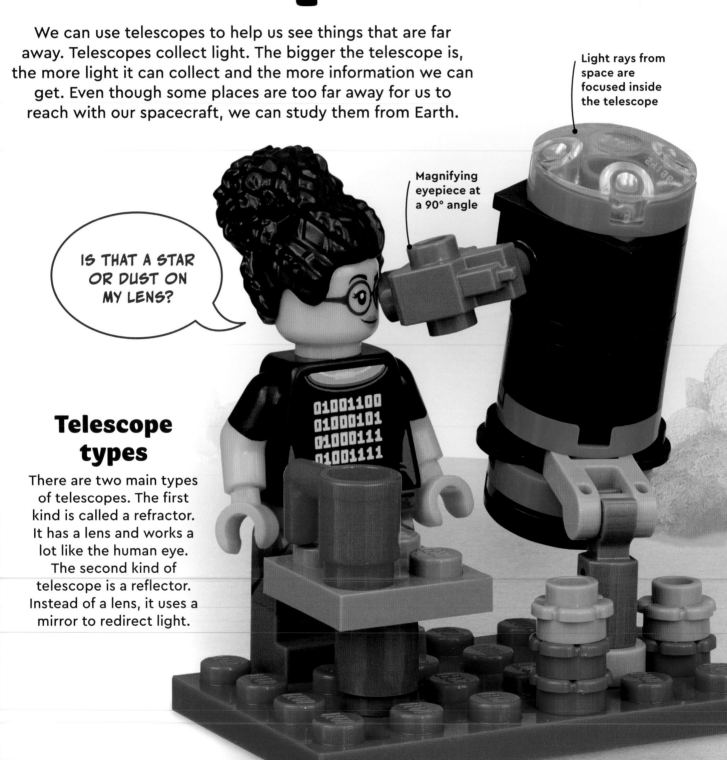

Light rays from space are focused inside the telescope

Magnifying eyepiece at a 90° angle

IS THAT A STAR OR DUST ON MY LENS?

Telescope types

There are two main types of telescopes. The first kind is called a refractor. It has a lens and works a lot like the human eye. The second kind of telescope is a reflector. Instead of a lens, it uses a mirror to redirect light.

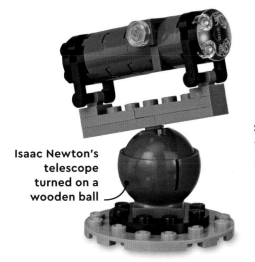

Isaac Newton's telescope turned on a wooden ball

The first telescopes

The first telescopes were made in 1608 CE; the following year, a scientist named Galileo used one to look at the sky. He discovered amazing things, like the fact that Jupiter has moons, the sun has spots, and our moon is covered in mountains and craters.

WOW!
With a backyard telescope you can see the **moons of Jupiter** just like Galileo—and maybe make some discoveries of your own!

Did you know?

The first minifigures to carry telescopes were **LEGO® Pirates**, in 2009. Pirates looked to the stars to navigate their ships at night, but mostly used telescopes to spot far-off ships on the horizon.

BUILD IT!
This build has a lift-off dome for access to the telescope. The scope can be lowered when not in use, and the roof hatch closed. When it is raised, there is room for a minifigure stargazer inside.

Sideways 6×6 curved round corner brick

Smooth tiles top the walls

Scope in lowered position

On a big scale

The world's biggest telescopes use mirrors built from many combined segments to collect light. These are protected inside large observatories. Scientists use these telescopes to study everything from comets in our solar system to distant galaxies.

Roof hatch closes up when telescope is not in use

Dome protects telescope from wind, rain, and dust

REALLY!
The Extremely Large Telescope in the Chilean Atacama Desert will be the biggest in the world when completed in about 2028. Its main mirror will be nearly as wide as **three** school buses end to end!

What is the most powerful telescope?

The James Webb Space Telescope is the largest telescope humans have ever sent into space. The bigger the telescope, the more detailed pictures it can make of stars, planets, and other space objects! Telescopes in space give a clearer image than telescopes on Earth because Earth's air can affect the light and blur what we see.

REALLY!
To function correctly, the James Webb Space Telescope must stay below **-370°F (-223°C)!**

Infrared light

The James Webb Space Telescope can see in a type of light called infrared. Humans cannot see infrared, but we can still learn a lot by using this type of light. Cameras and other devices collect and study the light to reveal the secrets of planets and to detect faraway galaxies.

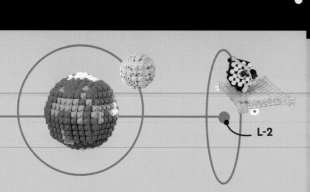

L-2

THIS TELESCOPE IS THE GOLD STANDARD.

L-2

The James Webb Space Telescope is in a special spot in space called L-2. L-2 is about four times as far away from Earth as the moon is from Earth. It orbits around the sun at the same speed as Earth.

Mirror, mirror

The big yellow panels on the James Webb Space Telescope are mirrors made out of the rare elements beryllium and gold. These elements were used because beryllium is very strong and gold is good at reflecting infrared light.

Did you know?

In 1990, NASA (the US National Aeronautics and Space Administration) launched the Hubble Space Telescope from a shuttle orbiting Earth. **LEGO® Icons NASA Space Shuttle Discovery (set 10283)** celebrates this launch with highly detailed models of both.

The large gold mirror is 21 ft (6.5 m) wide

WOW!
The James Webb Space Telescope is more than **100 times** more powerful than the Hubble Space Telescope.

Arm holding up secondary mirror

BUILD IT!

This model is built around a framework of long bars with end studs arranged into a diamond shape. Clips connect the inner surface to the bars and the tilting mirror.

1×2 plate with bar

1×1 tile with clip

1×1 plate with clip

Long bar with end studs

Shield protects mirrors from the sun's heat

33

How can we learn about things that are far away?

Scientists have to come up with lots of clever ways to learn about the universe. They can use tools like telescopes to help them see distant objects. They can send spacecraft to take photos and measurements of faraway planets, and they can do experiments in the laboratory to compare how things work on Earth with how they work in space.

Scanning equipment

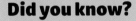
Did you know?

LEGO® Ideas Women of NASA (set 21312) celebrates four scientists who have added to our knowledge of the universe: astronomer Nancy Grace Roman, computer scientist Margaret Hamilton, and astronauts Sally Ride and Mae Jemison.

Space souvenirs

A sample return is when astronauts or robotic missions bring pieces of things from space, like asteroids or the moon, back to Earth. Sample returns help scientists figure out how and when these objects formed.

Large telescope for viewing faint objects

BUILD IT!

The angled sides of the prism tilt inward on hinge bricks. The flat base is built sideways, stretching out from back-to-back headlight bricks, with pairs of 1×1 slopes at both ends.

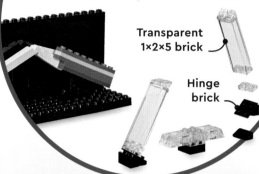

Transparent 1×2×5 brick

Hinge brick

Over the rainbow

Objects in space can give off light, absorb light, or reflect light. Scientists can split an object's light into its separate colors with prisms to learn more about it, such as what it is made of and how fast it is moving. This is called spectroscopy.

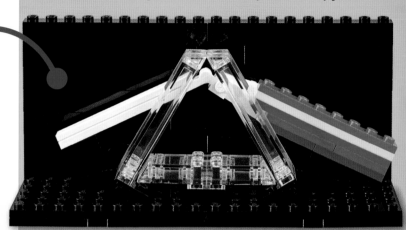

Collection of rock samples

WOW!
Helium was first discovered in the sun using spectroscopy.

Studying space

There are lots of different kinds of scientists who study space! Scientists who learn about planets are called planetary scientists, scientists who study stars are called stellar astronomers, and scientists who explore ideas like how the universe was born are called cosmologists.

THINK I'M GONNA NEED SOME MORE SHELVES...

REALLY!
The Apollo missions brought back **842 pounds** (382 kg) of rock from the moon!

How can robots help us learn about space?

We use robots to go to places in our solar system where it is currently too dangerous to send a human, or it would take too long. Some robotic spacecraft or probes fly by an object and send back photos, while others might orbit or even land on it. Scientists can control the craft from Earth, but they have to be patient. Sometimes it can take many years to get there!

REALLY!
It took NASA's New Horizons mission **nine and a half years** to get to Pluto!

A new dawn

The *Dawn* spacecraft was an orbiter mission, launched in 2007. It was the first mission ever to orbit two different bodies. It first went to the asteroid Vesta and then to the dwarf planet Ceres.

The *Dawn* spacecraft had solar panels to provide power

Asteroid analysis

Hayabusa2 was a Japanese probe that landed rovers on the asteroid Ryugu in 2018 and brought back pieces to Earth to study. The mission was the first time a rover explored an asteroid.

ETA FOR LANDING? SEVEN YEARS!

IMAGINE!
What would your **LEGO space robot** look like? What would it collect or find?

BUILD IT!

You can make a model of the *Dawn* spacecraft with just a few small pieces! Start with a brick with four side studs, then add bars and tiles with clips to make the solar arrays.

1×1 brick with four side studs

Bar with stopper

1×1 tile with clip

Did you know?

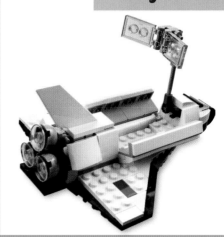

The satellite in **LEGO® Creator Space Shuttle (set 31134)** is made from just seven pieces! It fits inside a shuttle model measuring 5 inches (12 cm), which can be rebuilt as an astronaut or a futuristic interceptor craft.

A radio to talk with Earth

Ion thruster for speeding up the spacecraft

WOW!

Mariner 4 was the first **successful mission** in the Mariner program.

Mars mission

Mariner 4 was NASA's first mission to Mars. The probe flew by the red planet in 1965 and snapped the first close-up images of its surface. The photos showed that Mars was covered in craters, just like Earth's moon.

37

How does a Mars rover work?

Rovers are robotic vehicles that can explore the surface of a planet or space object. Scientists send rovers to learn as much as they can about places like the moon, Mars, or asteroids. The rovers have scientific instruments, such as sample collectors and cameras, to gather data. If the scientists see something interesting in the photos taken, they can tell the rover to drive closer or take more photos.

Camera rotates 360°

Hazcams help the rover navigate around hazards

REALLY!

NASA's Mars rover Opportunity was only designed to last **90 days**, but it kept going for more than **5,000 days!**

Space studies

Rovers let scientists study all kinds of things on Mars. They have explored craters, mountains, and rocky fields. The instruments, including radar, help people learn about the rocks, air, and weather on Mars.

SMILE! YOU'RE ON CAMERA!

Orbital periods

Mars and Earth both orbit around the sun, but Mars is farther away from the sun than Earth is so it has a longer orbital period (the time it takes to orbit). This means sometimes Earth and Mars are close to each other, and sometimes they are on opposite sides of the sun.

Mars

I'M OVER HERE!

Earth receives data via the rover's antenna

Mission to Mars

In 2020, NASA sent the rover Perseverance and a helicopter drone called Ingenuity to Mars. The landing site was a dried-up lake bed called Jezero Crater, where the rover searched for signs of past life.

Did you know?

LEGO® Technic NASA Mars Rover Perseverance (set 42158) is a motorized re-creation of the famous rover, complete with a mechanical arm, 360°-steering, suspension, and a replica Ingenuity drone!

WOW!
Ingenuity is the first aircraft to ever fly on **another planet**.

Tough wheels are essential for bumpy terrain

BUILD IT!
The four wheels on this microscale rover are round plates built on to 1×1 plates with rings. You can use any small parts to add complex-looking instruments on top.

1×2 jumper plate

1×1 plate with ring

IMAGINE!
What will your **LEGO rover** find on a distant planet? Build something unexpected!

39

How can we use radio waves to study space?

Radio waves are a type of light that is invisible to humans. Scientists and engineers build special telescopes, like the VLA (Very Large Array) to collect this type of light. Radio waves help scientists see through dust clouds in space, spot galaxies billions of light-years away, learn how hot something is, and tell if something has a magnetic field. We also use radio waves to communicate with spacecraft—even when they are very far from Earth!

Did you know?

In 2021, LEGO® Stores around the world displayed brick-built versions of photos taken by the Hubble Space Telescope, 7,000 light-years away from Earth! The images were received on Earth in the form of radio waves.

REALLY! Radio telescopes can be used during the **day** or **night**.

Forming a picture

Radio telescopes look like big bowls or dishes pointed at the sky. The radio waves hit the dish and are bounced into a smaller dish that then directs the light to a receiver. Scientists can use computers to turn the radio waves into a picture we can see with our eyes.

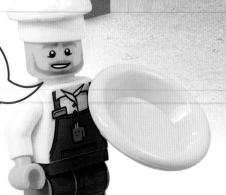

FANCY THE DISH OF THE DAY? OR MAYBE A FLYING SAUCER?

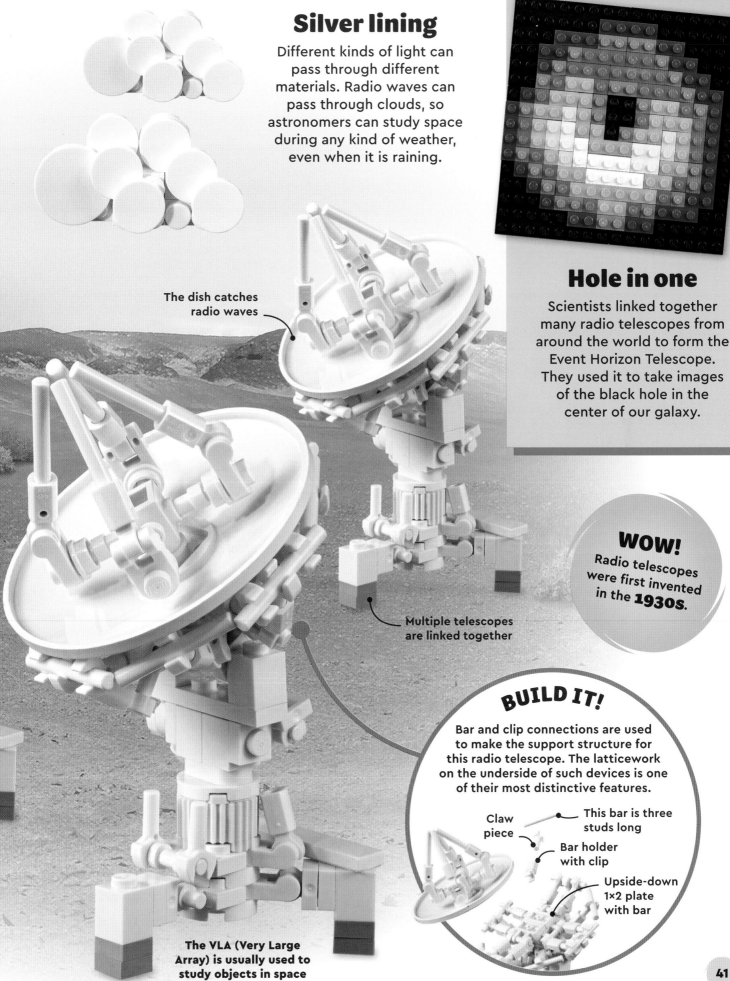

Silver lining

Different kinds of light can pass through different materials. Radio waves can pass through clouds, so astronomers can study space during any kind of weather, even when it is raining.

Hole in one

Scientists linked together many radio telescopes from around the world to form the Event Horizon Telescope. They used it to take images of the black hole in the center of our galaxy.

The dish catches radio waves

Multiple telescopes are linked together

WOW!
Radio telescopes were first invented in the **1930S**.

BUILD IT!

Bar and clip connections are used to make the support structure for this radio telescope. The latticework on the underside of such devices is one of their most distinctive features.

Claw piece

This bar is three studs long

Bar holder with clip

Upside-down 1×2 plate with bar

The VLA (Very Large Array) is usually used to study objects in space

Our Space Neighbors

Earth is one of many diverse worlds circling the sun. Some are blanketed in storms and have no solid ground to land on, while others are covered in glaciers with volcanoes that erupt ice. Many have surfaces carved by hundreds of impact craters. The solar system is full of adventure and discoveries waiting to be had. There could even be life beyond our planet!

How hot is the sun?

CHILE? I'M QUITE HOT ACTUALLY!

The sun is really hot! It's a sizzling ball of gas and the hottest thing in our solar system. It has several layers and no solid surface. Its surface is around 10,000°F (5,500°C), but it's even hotter inside! The sun's hottest layer is its core. If you could stick a thermometer into the core, it would read around 27 million °F (15 million °C)!

REALLY!
It takes light a little over eight minutes to travel the **93 million miles** (150 million km) between the sun and Earth.

Making energy

The sun is so massive that its weight crushes down on its core. The more the sun crushes inward, the hotter it becomes. There is so much heat and pressure at the core that tiny particles called hydrogen nuclei smash together to build other elements and release energy. This process is called nuclear fusion. The energy released by the sun reaches Earth as heat and light.

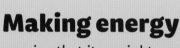

The surface of the sun is covered in bubbles of hot gas

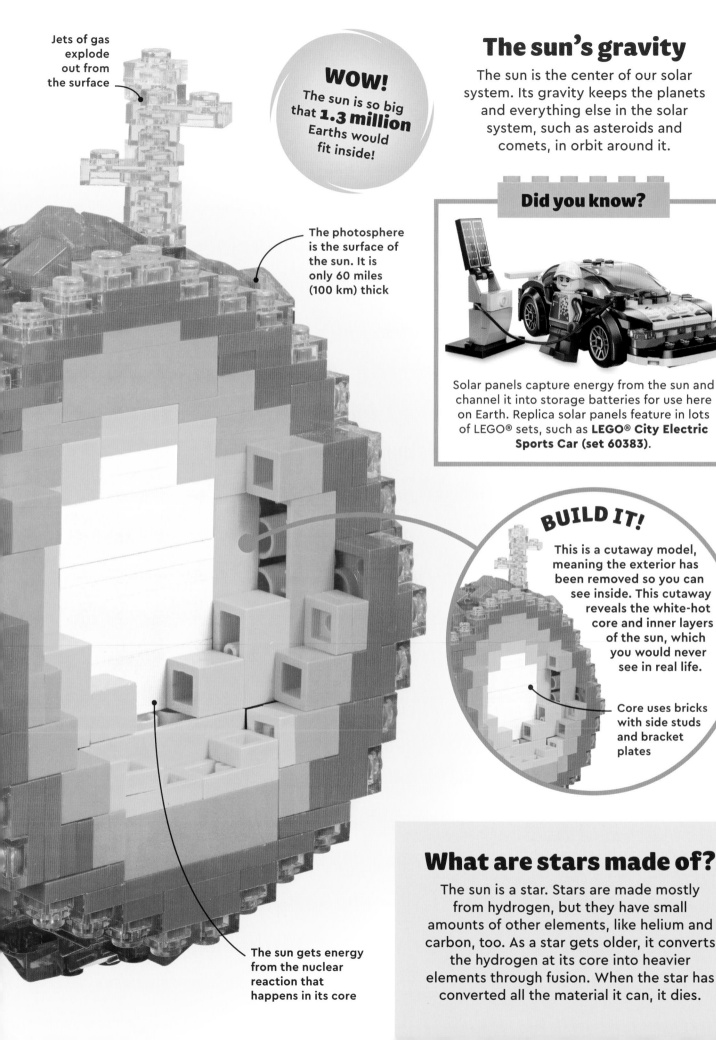

Jets of gas explode out from the surface

WOW!
The sun is so big that **1.3 million** Earths would fit inside!

The photosphere is the surface of the sun. It is only 60 miles (100 km) thick

The sun's gravity

The sun is the center of our solar system. Its gravity keeps the planets and everything else in the solar system, such as asteroids and comets, in orbit around it.

Did you know?

Solar panels capture energy from the sun and channel it into storage batteries for use here on Earth. Replica solar panels feature in lots of LEGO® sets, such as **LEGO® City Electric Sports Car (set 60383)**.

BUILD IT!

This is a cutaway model, meaning the exterior has been removed so you can see inside. This cutaway reveals the white-hot core and inner layers of the sun, which you would never see in real life.

Core uses bricks with side studs and bracket plates

The sun gets energy from the nuclear reaction that happens in its core

What are stars made of?

The sun is a star. Stars are made mostly from hydrogen, but they have small amounts of other elements, like helium and carbon, too. As a star gets older, it converts the hydrogen at its core into heavier elements through fusion. When the star has converted all the material it can, it dies.

Just how **big** do planets get?

Jupiter, Saturn, Uranus, and Neptune are the four giant planets in our solar system and are known as the Jovian planets. They are mostly made of gas, so unlike terrestrial or dwarf planets they have no solid surfaces to stand on. The biggest giant planet is Jupiter, which is 11 times wider than Earth. It has as much mass (is made up of as much stuff) as 318 Earths. As massive as Jupiter is, scientists think planets outside of our solar system may be up to 13 times more massive!

WOW!
It might **rain diamonds** on Saturn! Lightning turns methane into soot, which hardens into graphite, then diamonds.

Building blocks

The smallest piece of an element is an atom. Atoms can be stuck together like LEGO bricks to make molecules. Molecules are tiny pieces of chemicals. Molecules like ammonia and methane give the Jovian planets their particular colors.

Saturn's creamy clouds are ice cold

Saturn

Uranus has 13 rings

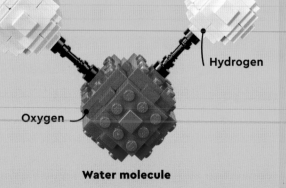

Hydrogen

Oxygen

Water molecule

Uranus

Jupiter's layers

The outer layer of Jupiter is made mostly of hydrogen gas. Giant storms whip around the surface, and below these storms, the temperature and pressure rise. The hydrogen gas is squeezed into a boiling hot liquid. The deeper inside Jupiter, the hotter it is. Eventually, the liquid hydrogen is squeezed and heated so hot it becomes metallic hydrogen.

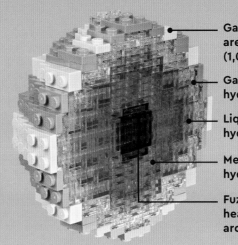

Gas and clouds are 600 miles (1,000 km) thick

Gaseous hydrogen

Liquid hydrogen

Metallic hydrogen

Fuzzy core of heavy elements around center

Jupiter spins so fast that its equator bulges outward

REALLY!
The center of Jupiter is about **43,000°F (24,000°C)!**

Did you know?

The classic LEGO® Space logo is inspired by Saturn and its rings—only here the ring effect is created by a spaceship whizzing out of orbit! It is worn by minifigures such as **Space Creature (set 71032-11).**

Jupiter

Neptune has the fastest-moving winds in the solar system

OH! THERE ARE *FOUR* GIANT PLANETS!

Zooming in

Neptune is unique among the Jovian planets in that it can only be seen with a telescope. If you go somewhere very dark and you know where to look, you can actually see Uranus without a telescope!

Neptune

Why does Pluto have a giant heart?

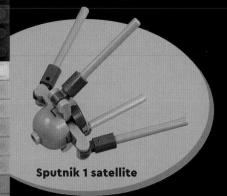
Sputnik 1 satellite

Pluto is a dwarf planet in the outer solar system that appears to have an enormous heart on its surface! Planetary scientists think that this heart may be an impact crater from a large object that smashed into its surface billions of years ago. The heart is named Tombaugh Regio after the discoverer of Pluto. The western lobe of the heart, Sputnik Planitia, is named after Sputnik 1, the first satellite in space.

Icy cold

Pluto orbits around the sun about 40 times farther away than Earth does. Because Pluto is so far away from the sun, its surface is hundreds of degrees below freezing! The mountains and rocks are made from ice and it can get so cold that the air freezes and snows onto the ground.

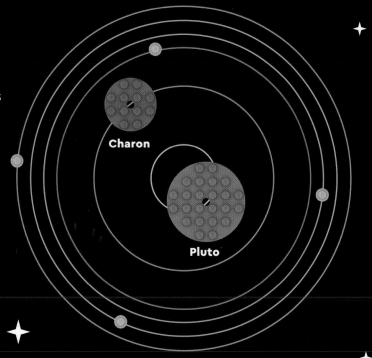
Charon

Pluto

Did you know?

Ninja Zane has never been to Pluto (so far as we know), but in **LEGO® NINJAGO® Castle of the Forsaken Emperor (set 70678)** he finds himself stranded in another far-off, frozen world!

Charon

Charon is Pluto's largest moon. It is so big compared to Pluto that many scientists consider Pluto and Charon to be a double planet (when two planets orbit around each other). Pluto and Charon have four smaller moons that orbit around them.

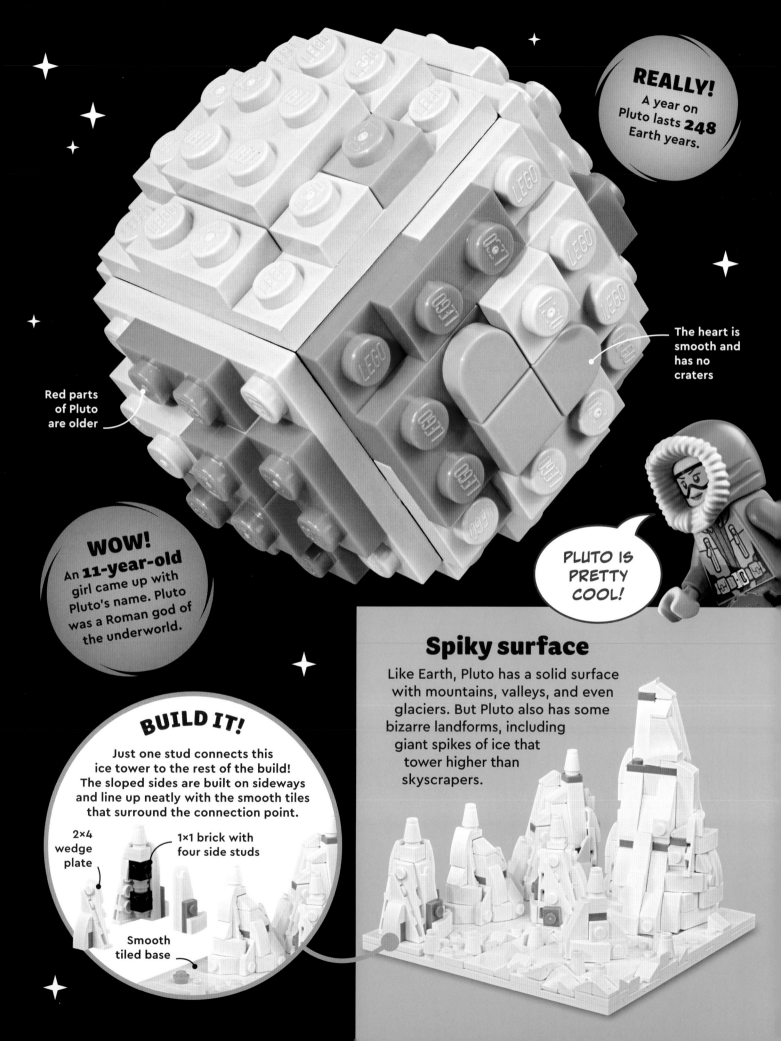

The heart is smooth and has no craters

Red parts of Pluto are older

PLUTO IS PRETTY COOL!

BUILD IT!

Just one stud connects this ice tower to the rest of the build! The sloped sides are built on sideways and line up neatly with the smooth tiles that surround the connection point.

2×4 wedge plate

1×1 brick with four side studs

Smooth tiled base

Spiky surface

Like Earth, Pluto has a solid surface with mountains, valleys, and even glaciers. But Pluto also has some bizarre landforms, including giant spikes of ice that tower higher than skyscrapers.

Could you go diving on **other** worlds?

Earth is the only planet we know of with oceans of liquid water on its surface. But it isn't the only world in our solar system with oceans! Many moons and dwarf planets have vast bodies of water hiding below thick layers of rock or ice. These are called Interior Water Ocean Worlds (IWOWs). We know of more than a dozen IWOWs ready to explore!

Plumes of water escape from cracks in the ice

Scientists are still investigating what the orange streaks on Europa's surface are

Europa

Europa is the smallest of Jupiter's four largest moons. Under its ice crust, the moon is covered in a thick liquid water ocean. Some scientists think there may be volcanoes and hot vents under the ocean, just like on Earth.

A thick layer of ice protects the ocean below

A liquid water ocean is under the ice

Volcanic activity might keep the water warm

Hydrothermal vents might be a place to search for life

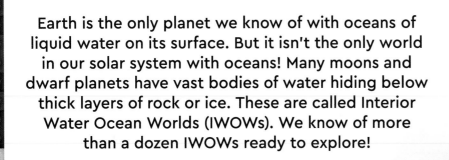

Transparent 1×6×5 wall piece

BUILD IT!

Transparent wall pieces make a window into this watery world. The cross-section model shows what a slice of IWOW would look like if you could remove it without the water falling out!

Digging deep

We can explore ocean worlds using photos taken by probes. But one day, planetary scientists hope to land probes on these worlds and drill into the oceans below. The probes would need to be able to drill and swim.

REALLY!
Even though Europa is smaller than Earth, it has **twice** as much water as all of Earth's oceans combined!

Meteors cause impacts on the icy surface

Titan

Titan is Saturn's largest moon. It is an IWOW on the inside but also has another liquid on its surface. Methane is normally a gas on Earth, but on Titan it is so cold that methane can be liquid or solid! Titan's rivers, lakes, and seas are made of liquid methane.

Chunks of ice form interesting shapes on the surface

WOW!
Titan is the only place outside the inner solar system we have landed a **space probe**.

I THOUGHT THE TRAVEL ITINERARY SAID "DIVING IN EUROPE."

Under the water is a rocky interior

Can a volcano erupt ice?

Scientists have discovered volcanoes that don't spew molten rock. They erupt with chemicals called ices, like water and ammonia, instead! They are called cryovolcanoes. Ahuna Mons, on the dwarf planet Ceres, is the closest known cryovolcano to Earth. It is about 200 million years old and stands half as tall as Earth's highest mountain, Mount Everest. It once poured ices out onto the surface of Ceres like lava flows on Earth.

WOW!
"Cryo" comes from the Greek word for **cold** or **ice**.

The frost line

The farther away from the sun an area of the solar system is, the colder it is. Cryovolcanoes are only found on objects beyond what is called the frost line. This is the distance away from the sun where it is cold enough for water to be frozen all of the time.

REALLY!
Cryovolcanoes might be a good place to search for **alien life**!

Did you know?

In **LEGO® Friends Igloo Holiday Adventure (set 41760)** there are thankfully no ice volcanoes in sight. There's a wintry waterfall instead, and an igloo made with transparent dome pieces.

Blow hot and cold

On Earth, lava is made mostly from molten silicon and oxygen. However, cryovolcano lava is made from ices such as water, ammonia, and methane. Even though they are called ices, they are liquid when they erupt.

Cracks and ridges on the crust of Ceres

Water, ammonia, and methane erupt out of the cryovolano

Cold cases

Planetary scientists have found what look like cryovolcanoes on many other worlds, including Europa, Enceladus, Triton, and Pluto. Cryovolcanoes may turn out to be very common in the solar system.

IMAGINE!

What might an **alien** look like on a frozen planet? Build a LEGO alien to discover!

BUILD IT!

Most of this cryovolcano plume is built upside down. The lowest upside-down part is a 2×2 round brick, which slots onto a bar. The bar also helps strengthen the base of the plume.

Upside-down 2×2 round brick

Bar

1×1 round brick

Salt deposits and mud created the mountain

FINALLY A VOLCANO I CAN GET ON BOARD WITH...

Ahuna Mons

Why do comets have tails?

Comets are made of ice and rock. Like everything else in the solar system, they orbit around the sun. When comets get close to the sun, their ices heat up and break apart, creating a tail. Most comets are really far away from the sun in the Kuiper Belt and the Oort Cloud, but a few comets come into the inner solar system where Earth is. When they get close enough we can see them in the sky.

WOW!
The word "comet" comes from the Greek word for **hair** because the ancients thought a comet looked like a star with a long ponytail!

The long and the short of it

Comets that take less than 200 years to orbit the sun are called short-period comets. Those that take more than 200 years are called long-period comets.

The head of a comet is known as the nucleus

REALLY!
Some comets can be as big as **cities**!

A cloud of dust and ice around the nucleus is called the coma

Comet landing

Comets formed when the solar system was very young, and haven't changed much since. So by studying comets, scientists can learn what the solar system was like 4.5 billion years ago. In 2004, the European Space Agency (ESA) sent the Rosetta mission to land on a comet called 67P/Churyumov-Gerasimenko.

Gas tail can be millions of miles in length

BUILD IT!

The core of this comet is built in the same way as the planets on page 17. Because it has studs on all sides, the long tail can be built off the comet in the same way as you would build a tower.

Dust tail reflects sunlight and appears white or yellow

Cosmic mystery

'Oumuamua is a mysterious object from another star that passed through our solar system in 2017. Some scientists suggest it could have been a piece of alien technology, but most think it was probably just a stray comet.

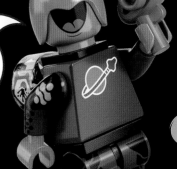

I'M EXHAUSTED. BEEN CHASING MY TAIL ALL DAY!

Why is Jupiter striped?

Jupiter's stripes are cold, windy clouds floating in its air, or atmosphere. Jupiter has no land, so winds whip around at hundreds of miles per hour, forming mostly uniform stripes because there is no land to slow them down. Jupiter's dark stripes are called belts and the lighter stripes are called zones. The belts form from cool air sinking, while the zones are made of warmer air rising from its hot interior. Neighboring Saturn is striped for the same reasons!

REALLY!
More than **1,300** Earths could fit inside Jupiter.

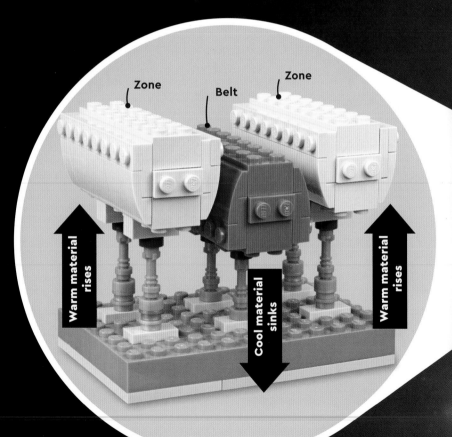

Zone

Belt

Zone

Warm material rises

Cool material sinks

Warm material rises

Colorful chemicals

Jupiter and Saturn are giant planets made almost entirely from two gases: hydrogen and helium. They get their colors from small amounts of chemicals like ammonia, sulfur, and phosphorus.

WOW!
Jupiter's Great Red Spot is a gigantic storm that has lasted for at least **300** years!

Pioneer 11 took the first close-up images of the Great Red Spot in 1974

There are three LEGO minifigures orbiting Jupiter! They got there on the NASA space probe Juno, and are made from aluminum. They are Jupiter (the god of sky and thunder and king of gods in Roman mythology), his wife Juno with a magnifying glass of discovery, and the 17th-century astronomer Galileo Galilei.

BY JUPITER, THAT'S A BIG DOWNPOUR!

Weather forecast

On Earth, weather is driven by heat from the sun. But Jupiter and Saturn are both far away from the sun and don't get much heat. Instead, their weather is powered by heat coming from deep inside the planets.

Exploring Saturn

There is a lot of data about Saturn's storms, rings, and moons. The *Cassini* spacecraft orbited around Saturn for 13 years, between 2004 and 2017. As well as collecting data, it took pictures of the planet.

Where's the biggest volcano in space?

Earth isn't the only planet with volcanoes! Olympus Mons on Mars is the largest volcano we know of in the solar system. Even though Mars is a smaller world than Earth, Olympus Mons is bigger than any mountain on our planet. It is three times the height of Mount Everest, and its base is so big it would cover the state of Arizona!

Olympus Mons is made from layers of solidified lava

BUILD IT!

Flame piece

1×1 round plate

1×2 plate

Flame pieces slot in to 1×1 round plates with open studs to make this volcanic landscape. If you don't have any flame pieces, build your own eruptions using red, yellow, and orange parts.

ALL THIS TALK OF VOLCANOES... I'M FIT TO EXPLODE.

A volcanic moon

One of Jupiter's moons, Io, is covered in erupting volcanoes. It is the most volcanically active world in the solar system, and its eruptions can be seen from space. Io's largest volcano, Loki Patera, is named after the Norse god Loki.

Valles Marineris

Not only does Mars have the largest known volcano, it also has the largest canyon in the solar system! Valles Marineris is five times as long and four times as deep as the Grand Canyon in Arizona.

Summit has six calderas (collapsed craters)

Olympus Mons is a broad volcano known as a shield volcano

Record-breaker

Mauna Kea in Hawaii is the biggest volcano on Earth. It is also the tallest mountain, at 32,000 ft (9,750 m) from its base to its peak. However, most of it is under the water, so we can't see all of it.

Did you know?

Instead of using a printed instruction book, **LEGO® City Mars Spacecraft Exploration Missions (set 60354)** is designed to be built using a smartphone adventure app that takes you all the way to Mars!

What is the asteroid belt?

Asteroids are chunks of rock and metal that orbit the sun, and they are usually uneven in shape. There are millions of asteroids in our solar system, and most of the known ones are located in the asteroid belt, a vast ring of debris that orbits between Mars and Jupiter. "Asteroid" means "starlike" because although early astronomers knew asteroids were not stars, they looked like stars through small telescopes.

Asteroids in the belt are actually very far apart

DIDN'T EXPECT THIS JOURNEY TO BE SO ROCKY!

BUILD IT!

This spaceship's wings are more like an insect's than an airplane's! A single ball-and-socket joint connects each one at the front, allowing it to twist and turn to suit different conditions.

1×2 plate with ball

Sideways 1×2 plate with socket

Building blocks

Many asteroids are made from minerals that could be used for building spaceships or space stations in the future. Some asteroids even have water ice that could be used for drinking or making rocket fuel.

WOW!
Ceres is named after the **Roman goddess** of grain and agriculture. This is also where the word "cereal" comes from.

Some asteroids look like space potatoes!

Early discovery

Ceres was the first object ever discovered in the asteroid belt. It was spotted on January 1st, 1801. Dwarf planet Ceres is far bigger than any other asteroid. Planetary scientists suspect it may have formed in a different part of the system and moved to the asteroid belt billions of years ago.

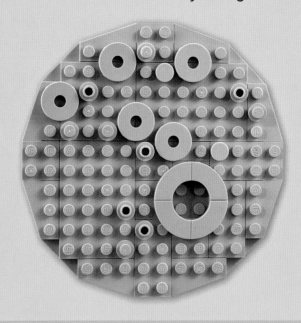

Did you know?

Passengers on the **LEGO® City Space Ride Amusement Truck (set 60313)** can imagine what it feels like to be an asteroid. They spin around and around in an unchanging orbit!

Home sweet asteroid

Vesta is the second largest asteroid. It is so large that planetary scientists believe it has an iron core and once had volcanoes on its surface. It could be a great location for a space base.

REALLY!
Vesta is the only asteroid visible from Earth without a **telescope!**

What is a shooting star?

Have you ever seen a shooting star? Also called meteors, shooting stars aren't really stars at all. They are actually bits of debris that fall to the ground from space. As the small pieces of rock or dust fall, they rub up against the air and get so hot they burn up.

A meteor moves through the sky at about 45 miles (70 km) per second

BUILD IT!

Walls made from black bricks make a good backdrop for space models. Add stars by slotting white, bar-shaped pieces into headlight bricks from behind.

Headlight brick

Mechanical claw

Rear view

Raining meteors

When comets get close to the sun they can leave behind trails of debris. If Earth passes through the cloud of material left behind, there will be lots of meteors or shooting stars on the same night. When lots of meteors happen at the same time, it is called a meteor shower.

WOW!
One of the largest meteor showers of the year, called the **Perseids**, happens every August.

Deep impact

Sometimes very large objects like comets and asteroids hit Earth or other bodies in the solar system, like the moon or Mars. When the object hits the planet, it leaves behind a crater. The largest impact crater in the solar system is the South Pole-Aitken Basin, found on the moon.

I'M SURE MY GOLF BALL HEADED THIS WAY...

A bright trail comes from the meteor as it burns

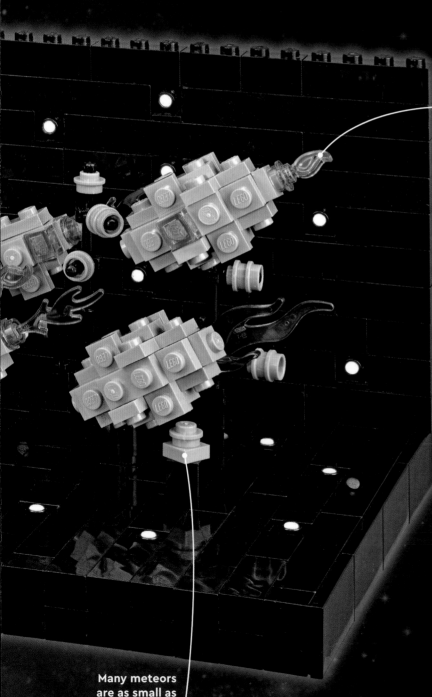

Many meteors are as small as pebbles

REALLY!
The South Pole-Aitken Basin is about **1,600 miles** (2,575 km) across.

Did you know?

LEGO® Creator Space Roller Coaster (set 31142) takes minifigures on a hair-raising ride past rockets, planets, a Martian rover, and a flaming meteor with a tail that really glows!

Burning rocks

Sometimes meteors don't completely burn up before they hit the ground. A rock that has fallen from space is called a meteorite. Every single day, 10 to 50 meteorites hit Earth. Most end up falling into the ocean, but sometimes explorers find them in open places like deserts or Antarctica.

What are Saturn's rings made of?

Saturn's rings may look like solid sheets, but they are actually made of millions and millions of tiny pieces of ice orbiting around the planet. The ice pieces can be as small as specks of dust or as big as houses. The ring particles are good at reflecting light, so they make Saturn look very bright.

WOW!
Saturn hasn't always had its rings. One day the rings will **disappear** again!

REALLY!
Saturn's rings measure a massive **175,000 miles** (280,000 km) across!

Did you know?

The rocket that first took astronauts to the moon in 1969 shares its name with the ringed planet. **LEGO® Ideas NASA Apollo Saturn V (set 21309)** recreates the historic vessel—in 1,969 pieces!

Ring formation

Scientists think Saturn got its rings when a moon made of ice orbited too close to the planet. Saturn's powerful gravity tore the moon into the little pieces that now make up its rings.

SATURN RUNS RINGS AROUND OTHER PLANETS!

Dwarf planets

Rings have been found around dwarf planets like Haumea. Haumea probably got its rings from a giant collision that knocked pieces of ice and rocks into orbit around it.

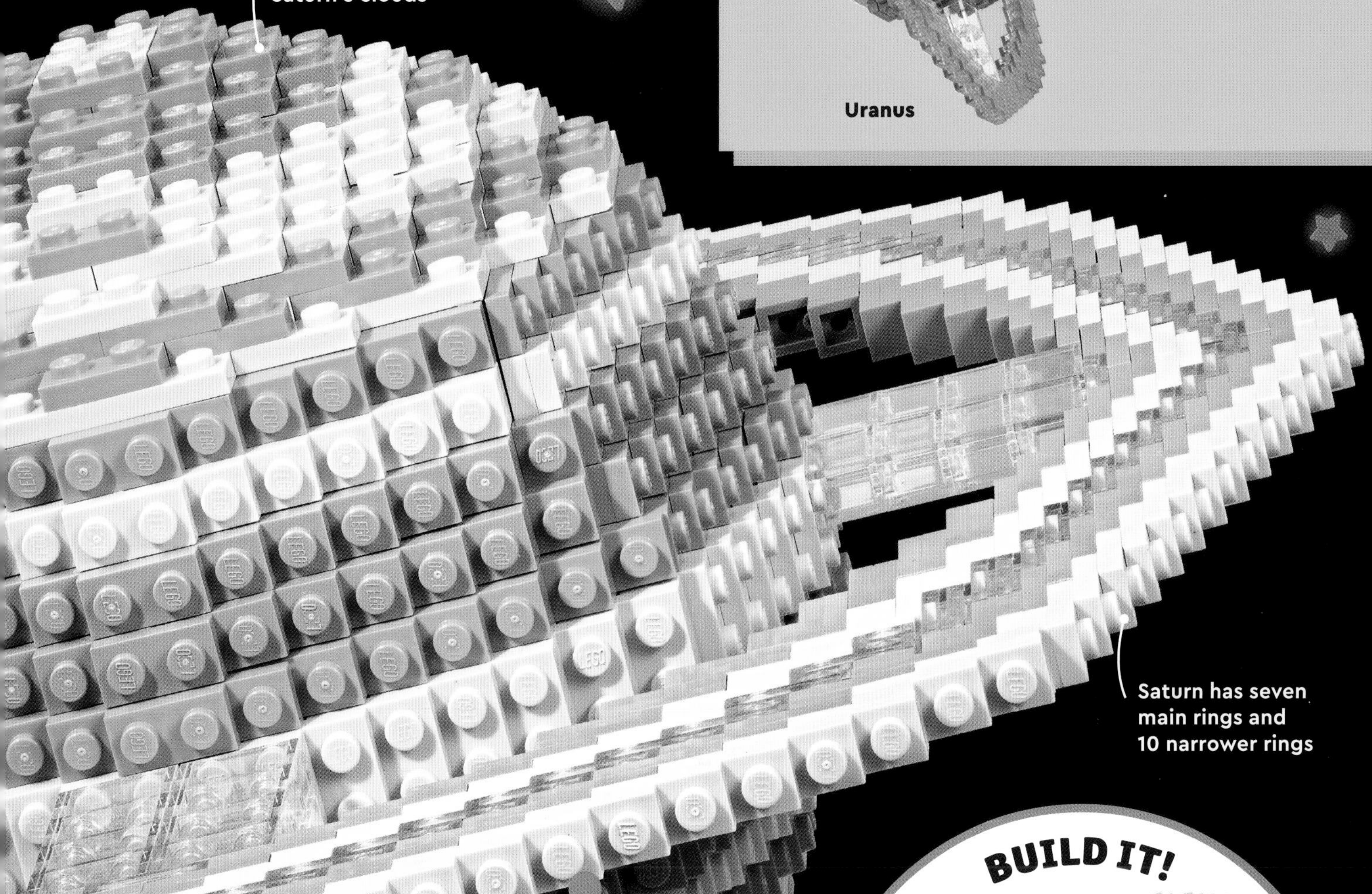

A thin layer of foggy haze covers Saturn's clouds

Giant planets

Saturn isn't the only giant planet with rings. Jupiter, Uranus, and Neptune all have rings, too. But their rings are hard to spot because they are made of rock and dust that doesn't reflect much light.

Uranus

Saturn has seven main rings and 10 narrower rings

BUILD IT!

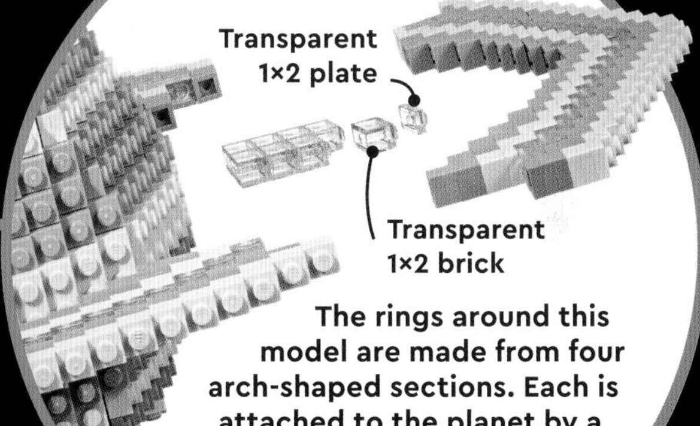

Transparent 1×2 plate

Transparent 1×2 brick

The rings around this model are made from four arch-shaped sections. Each is attached to the planet by a stack of transparent bricks, but the sections are not attached to each other.

Could you live on Venus?

NO NEED TO WRAP UP WARM TO GO TO VENUS.

Venus is one of Earth's closest neighbors. It is almost the same size and mass as Earth. However, Venus's surface is almost 900 °F (480 °C)—that's about three times as hot as the temperature at which you would bake cookies in the oven. Humans could not live or visit there without special equipment to protect them.

Hot off the press

Venus is covered in volcanoes! There are hundreds of them on its surface. Planetary scientists found that one of Venus's largest volcanoes, Maat Mons, is still active.

Scientific instruments help scientists learn about Venus

BUILD IT!

The top of the *Venera 9* orbiter gets its round shape from five radar dish pieces. Underneath them, two bracket plates and two inverted bracket plates add side studs all the way around a boxy core.

1×2/2×2 bracket plate

3×3 radar dish

2×2 round jumper plate

Solar panels power the *Venera 9*, the first craft to orbit Venus in 1975

A lot of Venus's surface is solid rock that used to be liquid

WOW!
Venus's **day** is longer than its **year**! It may have been hit by a large object that slowed its spin down.

DAVINCI+

Venusian voyage

NASA plans to send two uncrewed missions back to Venus—DAVINCI+ and VERITAS—by 2030. These missions will study the land and air of Venus, giving us clues as to why it is so different from Earth and whether life has ever existed, or currently exists, on it.

Did you know?

Venus has a swirling, cloudy atmosphere. You can create your own cloudy LEGO scenes with special cloud pieces like the ones seen in **LEGO® Creator Australia Postcard (set 40651).**

REALLY!
Venus is covered in **clouds**, so astronomers used to think it might be a wet, jungle world.

Venus's atmosphere

Venus is very hot because it has a super-thick atmosphere. Its air is almost 100 times as thick as Earth's air. However, we would not be able to breathe the air as it is mostly carbon dioxide. Carbon dioxide is a greenhouse gas that traps heat, so the planet stays very hot.

Could there be life beyond Earth?

Space is really, REALLY big! There are so many areas to explore. Scientists haven't found any life beyond Earth yet, but there are some great places in our solar system to look for it. Life might look very different on other planets. However we know that on Earth all life needs liquid water, so finding water in space might help us find life.

BUILD IT!

This icy alien has strong joints made from ball-and-socket joints, and fins made from teeth with clips instead of hands and feet. Tooth parts are also used to make its spiky head crest!

1×2 plate with bar

1×2 plate with ball socket

1×2 plate with ball

Tooth with clip

1×2 plate with clips

Life on Mars?

Billions of years ago, Mars may have been very similar to Earth. It used to have a thick atmosphere, warm temperatures, and liquid water flowing on its surface. Liquid water might still exist below the surface. Some scientists hope there could be simple life still hiding in this water.

SHHHH! YOU HAVEN'T SEEN ME!

A great atmosphere

The surface of Venus is too hot for water, but high above it there is a layer of cloud just the right temperature for liquid water. Some scientists think bacteria could float in Venus's clouds and use energy from the sun just like plants do on Earth.

EVER GET THE FEELING YOU'RE BEING WATCHED?

Below the surface

The oceans underneath thick layers of ice on worlds like Europa or Pluto would be perfect places to look for life. Who knows what kind of amazing creatures could be swimming around down there?

REALLY!
Microscopic **water bears**, also called tardigrades, have survived the vacuum of space!

Did you know?

LEGO City astronauts meet aliens in sets such as **LEGO® City Space Explorer Rover and Alien Life (set 60431)**. Each alien is made from three pieces, including a green minifigure head printed with three eyes!

IMAGINE!
What might an **alien's vehicle** look like on a frozen planet? Build a cool ride!

69

Where does the solar system stop?

The solar system is huge! Scientists don't know exactly how big it is yet, but they do know there is a lot more to explore. The most distant world visited by spacecraft is the planetesimal Arrokoth, which was spotted by the Hubble Space Telescope. Planetesimals are chunks of rock or ice that aren't quite big enough to be round planets. Arrokoth is made from two objects that bumped into each other, forming what looks like a red snowman!

WOW!
Arrokoth is 45 times farther from the sun than Earth. That's more than **4 billion miles** (6 billion km)!

BUILD IT!
An oilcan, a socket wrench, and a clockwork key element combine to make a complex-looking arrangement of tech on the end of this model. It is attached using bricks with side studs.

1×2 brick with side studs

6×6 round plate

Socket wrench

Communications antennas send information back to Earth

Solar panels create electricity to power the telescope

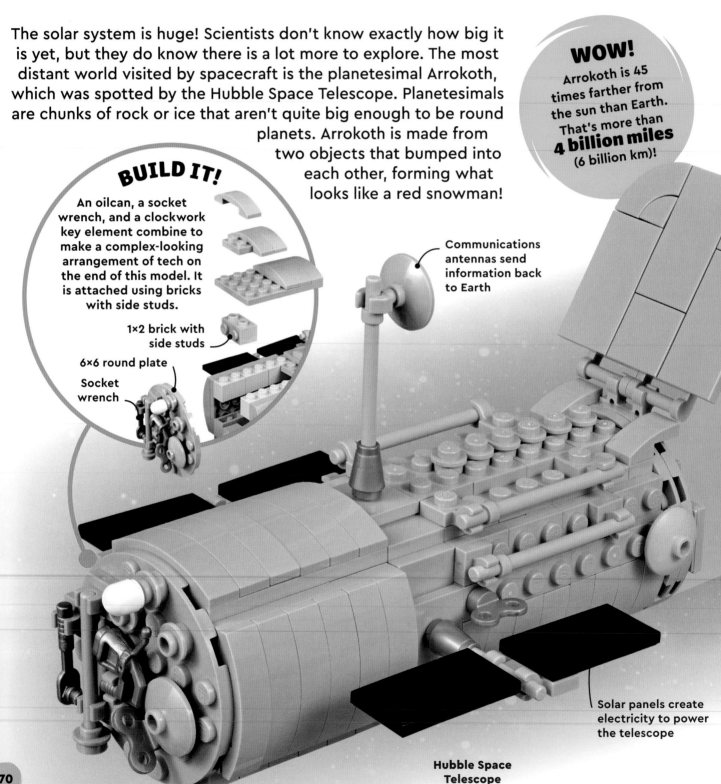

Hubble Space Telescope

Did you know?

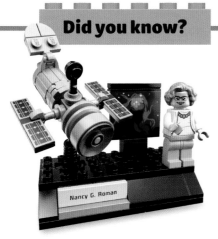

A microscale model of the Hubble Space Telescope appears in **LEGO® Ideas Women of NASA (set 21312)**. The model is made from 20 pieces, including one element that is usually used as a trash can!

Door closes to stop sunlight from damaging the telescope

Out there

One of the most distant places in our solar system is the dwarf planet Sedna. Sedna orbits so far away from the sun that it takes more than 11,000 years to go around just once!

AUNT ARROKOTH? IS THAT YOU?!

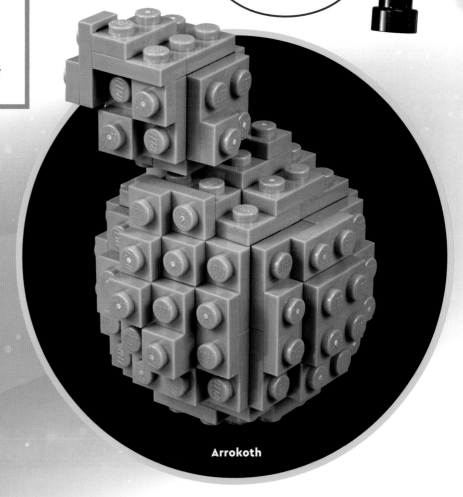

Arrokoth

Beyond Neptune

Neptune is the farthest giant planet from the sun, but there are more things in the system beyond Neptune. The Kuiper Belt is a ring of icy objects such as comets and dwarf planets. Beyond this, scientists think there is a comet-filled region called the Oort Cloud. It is shaped like a bubble surrounding the whole system.

REALLY!
The Oort Cloud may stretch as far as **1 light-year**!

Astronomical unit

When scientists talk about how far away something is in the solar system, they use a unit of distance called an astronomical unit. One astronomical unit is the same distance as Earth is from the sun. So if something is five astronomical units away from the sun, it is five times as far away as Earth is.

Which spacecraft are **farthest** from Earth?

Five spacecraft are currently headed out of the solar system: *Pioneer 10*, *Pioneer 11*, *Voyager 1*, *Voyager 2*, and *New Horizons*. *Voyager 1* is the farthest away, having reached a point more than 15 billion miles (24 billion km) from Earth! The *Voyagers* and *New Horizons* are still operational, and scientists use them to study the outer solar system. *New Horizons* launched most recently, in 2006, and should continue working into the late 2040s.

New Horizons antenna receives commands from Earth

The grand tour

In 1977, the twin spacecraft *Voyager 1* and *Voyager 2* launched. Over the next 12 years they visited all four giant planets of the solar system. *Voyager 2* is the only spacecraft to have ever flown by Uranus and Neptune!

REALLY!
Voyager 1 is traveling faster than **38,000 miles per hour** (61,000 kph)!

Distant objects

The sun creates a protective bubble around the solar system called the heliosphere, which helps protect planets like Earth from harmful radiation. The *Voyager* spacecraft have left the heliosphere, but they still have a long way to go before they pass the orbits of the most distant comets.

Voyager 1

Thermal generator powers the spacecraft

On the move

Spacecraft with high-quality cameras can help scientists back on Earth figure out how far away stars are. They use a method called stellar parallax. Scientists take photos of stars from Earth and compare them with photos taken by *New Horizons*. They measure how much the stars' directions change between the two points of view.

GLAD I PACKED THE LONG LENS!

Metal-coated plastic film regulates temperature

Beyond Our Sun

Beyond the icy outer solar system is a galaxy full of strange objects. There are stars that dwarf our sun, clouds of glowing gas and dust, black holes that swallow light, and the possibility of messages from alien civilizations. What mysteries of the Milky Way and beyond will you discover?

Where do stars come from?

Stars are huge balls of hydrogen that get so hot at their centers that they smash small particles called hydrogen nuclei together in a process called fusion. Fusion creates the heat and light we know as sunlight and starlight. Fusion can also create new elements, like helium and carbon. Stars are made when gravity pulls lots of hydrogen and other elements together. The more material squeezed into the star, the stronger the gravity becomes, and the hotter the star's center becomes.

Protostars

Before fusion begins in a star's center, it is called a protostar. "Proto" means early or before. So, a protostar is like a baby star.

Did you know?

You may be lucky to find stars in a LEGO® set! **LEGO® City The Knockdown Stunt Challenge (set 60341)** comes with seven star-shaped pieces that glow in the dark!

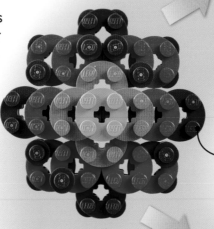

Stellar nebula

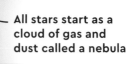

Stars like the sun are low-mass

Average star

All stars start as a cloud of gas and dust called a nebula

White dwarfs

Stars like the sun are low-mass stars. This means they don't have as much material as some big stars. Instead of exploding when they run out of fuel, low-mass stars push their outer layers off, forming a cloud of gas and dust called a planetary nebula. The core of the star left behind is called a white dwarf. Eventually material from the nebula may end up in new stars.

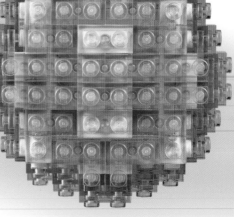

Massive stars glow blue to white

Massive star

REALLY! A star's center must reach a temperature of **millions of degrees** for fusion to happen.

How do stars die?

Eventually, stars will run out of material at their centers to fuse, and they die. When massive stars run out of fuel, they collapse in on themselves and explode outward in a giant explosion called a supernova. The material blasted into space can form nebulae that eventually collapse to create new stars.

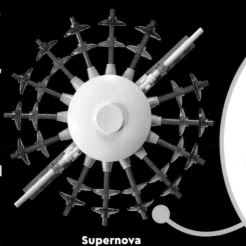

Supernova

BUILD IT!

This explosion of cosmic color is built around a large steering wheel piece. Claw pieces link each spur to the wheel, and a star-bright radar dish covers the connections in the center.

4×4 radar dish

2×2 radar dish

1×1 cone

Bar

Claw

Red giant

Old stars swell up and turn red

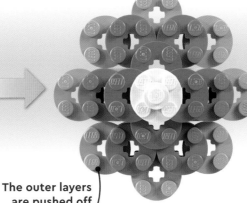

The outer layers are pushed off

Planetary nebula

The bright hot core is all that's left behind

White dwarf

WOW! The closest star to the sun is a **low-mass star** named Proxima Centauri.

Most massive stars turn into neutron stars when they die

Massive stars explode when they die

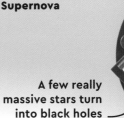

Supernova

Neutron star

Old massive stars get really big!

Red supergiant

A few really massive stars turn into black holes

Black hole

Are all stars the same?

Even though stars might look similar from the surface of Earth, they actually come in many different sizes and colors. The more matter a star is made of, the more massive it is. Massive stars get hotter at their centers than stars with less mass. The hotter the center of a star is, the faster it uses up its fuel and dies.

BUILD IT!

Stacking transparent colored parts on top of a different color can create interesting effects. Here, transparent yellow on solid red gives a sense of fiery heat trapped within.

Transparent yellow 1×1 and 1×2 plates

Red 1×1 brick with side stud

Stack of two red 2×2 plates

Our sun

The sun is a dwarf star, which means that compared to some stars it is very small. The largest known star, Stephenson 2–18, is more than 2,000 times the size of our sun.

WOW!
In about 5 **billion years,** our sun will turn into a red giant star.

Small red dwarfs are the most common kind of star

The sun is a yellow star

Wolf 359

The sun

Did you know?

You should never look directly at the sun, but you can look at the **LEGO® Technic Planet Earth and Moon in Orbit (set 42179).** The model shows Earth moving around the sun and the moon orbiting Earth.

DON'T THINK I'LL NEED TO USE THE FLASH!

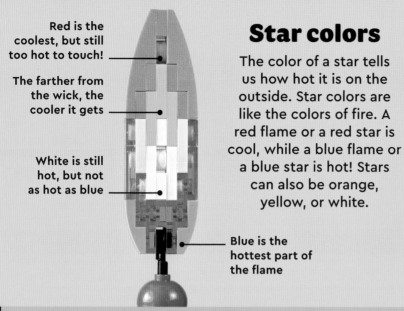

Star colors

The color of a star tells us how hot it is on the outside. Star colors are like the colors of fire. A red flame or a red star is cool, while a blue flame or a blue star is hot! Stars can also be orange, yellow, or white.

Red is the coolest, but still too hot to touch!

The farther from the wick, the cooler it gets

White is still hot, but not as hot as blue

Blue is the hottest part of the flame

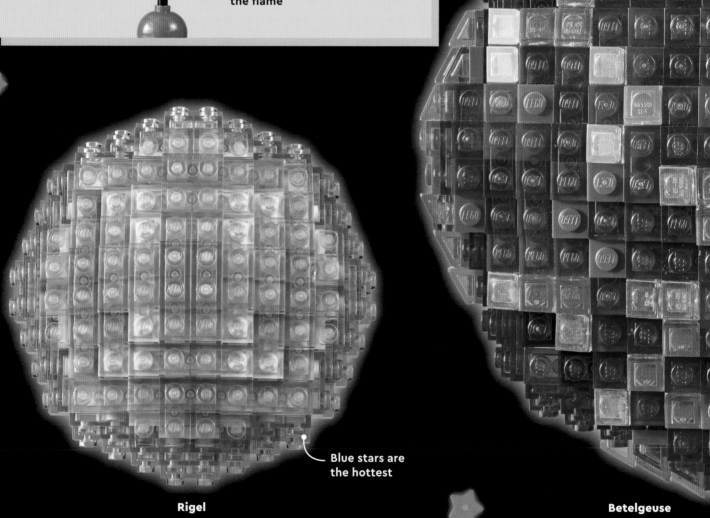

Old stars grow big and turn red

Blue stars are the hottest

Rigel

Betelgeuse

Bright lights

When we see stars from Earth, some of them look bright and others look dim. The amount of light a star gives off is called its luminosity, but it's the amount that reaches Earth that determines its brightness. Some very luminous stars do not look bright to us because they are very far away, and some not-very-luminous stars look bright to us because they are close by.

REALLY!
About **73 percent** of all stars in the galaxy are red dwarfs.

Why do stars twinkle?

In space, stars don't twinkle. But when you look at stars from Earth, they appear to do so. This is because we are looking at them through Earth's atmosphere where the air is very thick and moves around. As the light travels through the air, it gets distorted, making it seem as if the stars are twinkling. Telescopes in space are above the air, so they can get clearer images.

A cloudless night is best for spotting stars

Did you know?

A light brick in **LEGO® DUPLO 3in1 Space Shuttle Adventure (set 10422)** makes its special star piece extra twinkly! The set helps young builders learn about outer space and Earth's place in the universe.

A star's orbit

Most stars orbit around the center of their galaxies, just like planets orbit around stars. Because galaxies are so large, it can take stars millions of years to go around just once.

Open places without bright lights are good for stargazing

BUILD IT!

For this scene, star parts are built onto headlight bricks. Leaving the stars off and shining a light from behind creates a different starry effect through the holes in the headlight bricks.

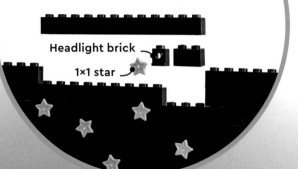

Headlight brick

1×1 star

Around and around

Many stars orbit around other stars. When two stars orbit around each other, they are called binary stars. It is not uncommon for stars to orbit in larger groups, too, like three or four stars in one system.

114, 115, 116... NO, I'VE LOST COUNT!

Telescopes can help you see even more stars

WOW!

One way to tell a planet from a star in the sky is that planets don't **twinkle** as much as stars appear to do.

Starry, starry night

Scientists don't know exactly how many stars there are in the universe. But there are probably around 250 billion stars in our galaxy, and there are hundreds of billions of galaxies we can see in the observable universe, each with their own hundreds of billions of stars! That's a LOT of stars!

REALLY!

The star system of Castor has **six stars** all orbiting around each other.

What happens if something falls into a **black hole?**

Black holes are places in space where the gravity is so strong that nothing can travel fast enough to escape. Before an object falls into a black hole, it is squeezed and squashed by the immense gravity. Sometimes the material falling into a black hole can swirl around it, giving off huge amounts of light before plunging beyond the point of no return, known as the event horizon.

BUILD IT!

The bands of this accretion disk are made by linking plates with end clips and plates with end bars. The outer band has 11 clip-and-bar connections, and the inner one has just five.

1×2 plate with clip

1×2 plate with bar

1×1 tile with clip

Amazing mass

Mass is how much matter is in an object, but size or volume is how much space it takes up. Black holes squeeze a huge amount of mass into a very small space. The more mass packed into an object, the stronger its gravity is.

Accretion disk is made of material swirling into the black hole

REALLY!

There is a **supermassive black hole** in the center of our galaxy called Sagittarius A*.

About time

The closer you get to a black hole, the slower time goes for you from the perspective of Earth. Time will feel normal to you, but for anyone watching you, it would look like you are in slow motion!

Anything that passes beyond the event horizon can't come back out!

WOW!

Scientists predicted the existence of black holes **decades** before finding them.

YIKES! I'M OUTTA HERE!

Wormholes

Tunnels that connect two different places or times in the universe are called wormholes. Scientists have not yet figured out whether these shortcuts exist, but some physicists think black holes could be hiding wormholes inside them.

Did you know?

There have been many astronaut minifigures over the years, but **LEGO® Minifigures (set 71037-3)** features the first to wear a brown space suit—and the very first **Spacebaby**!

What is the closest exoplanet?

Exoplanets are planets that don't orbit around our sun. Some exoplanets go around other stars, and some have lost their stars entirely and orbit the center of the galaxy. There are lots of different exoplanets—some are larger than Jupiter, while others are small and rocky like Earth. The closest known exoplanet is an Earth-sized planet called Proxima Centauri b.

WOW!
Some Earth-like exoplanets orbit so close to their star that their surfaces are **molten hot!**

Alpha Centauri

Proxima Centauri b's sun, Proxima Centauri, is part of the Alpha Centauri star system. This star system has two stars that are both like our sun—Alpha Centauri A and Alpha Centauri B. They orbit each other very closely and they are orbited by Proxima Centauri, a small red dwarf star. We know that Proxima Centauri has at least two planets orbiting it, but scientists aren't sure yet whether Alpha Centauri A and Alpha Centauri B have planets, too.

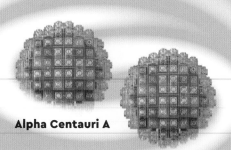

Alpha Centauri A

Alpha Centauri B

Proxima Centauri

The side facing away from the star is always cold

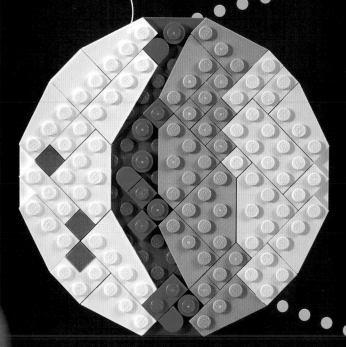

Proxima Centauri b

Proxima Centauri b

Proxima Centauri b is similar in size to Earth but orbits its star, Proxima Centauri, so closely that one side of the planet is locked facing the star while the other faces away. One side is in permanent day while the other is in permanent night.

In the distance

Planets are tiny compared to stars! Because exoplanets are so much smaller than their stars and so far from our solar system it can be difficult to spot them. Proxima Centauri b is a little over 4 light-years away—that is almost 24 trillion miles (40 trillion kilometers).

Did you know?

Proxima Centauri is part of the Centaurus constellation, named for its resemblance to a mythical centaur. The half-human, half-horse **Centaur Warrior** appears as a minifigure in **LEGO® Minifigures (set 71029-6)**.

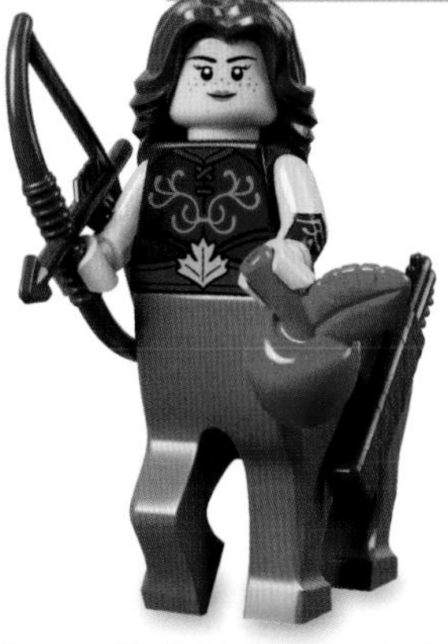

REALLY!
Scientists have found more than **5,000** exoplanets!

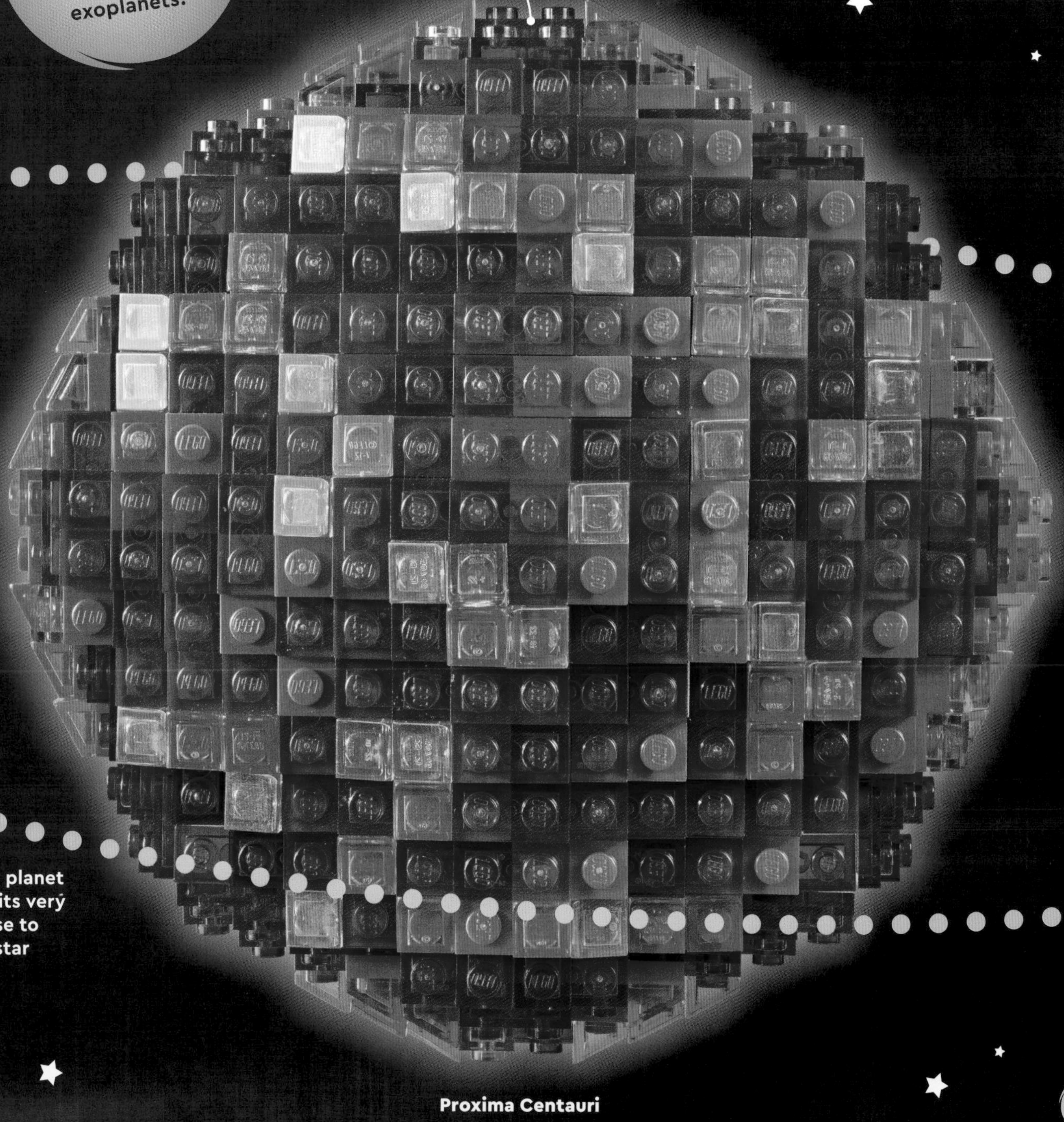

Proxima Centauri is a small red star
The planet orbits very close to its star

Proxima Centauri

Could we send a message to aliens?

Scientists don't know yet if there is life beyond Earth, let alone if there are other intelligent civilizations out there. If there are, maybe we could find them and send a message saying hello. SETI is the Search for Extraterrestrial Intelligence. SETI scientists have come up with many clever way to look for aliens.

REALLY!
In the **1950S**, scientists began to wonder if we could detect radio signals from aliens.

Radio receiver is suspended above the dish

Arecibo radio telescope

Radio dish has a diameter of 1,000 feet (305 m)

Is anyone there?

Radio waves are a form of light, or electromagnetic radiation, that humans can't see. We can use radio telescopes to observe things in space, like stars and galaxies. Some scientists hope that if alien civilizations use radio waves, maybe we will be able to find them with radio telescopes, like the Arecibo telescope, which was active until 2020.

Did you know?

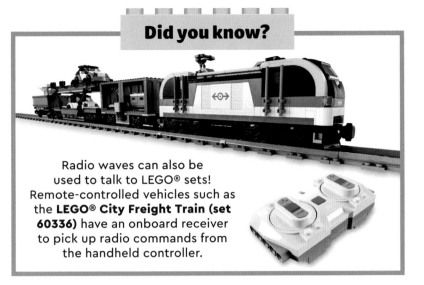

Radio waves can also be used to talk to LEGO® sets! Remote-controlled vehicles such as the **LEGO® City Freight Train (set 60336)** have an onboard receiver to pick up radio commands from the handheld controller.

Telescope sits in dip in a hillside

BUILD IT!

This re-creation of the Arecibo message is made as a mosaic, using smooth tiles. The flat model is built on a base of large plates, measuring 23 studs wide and 73 studs long.

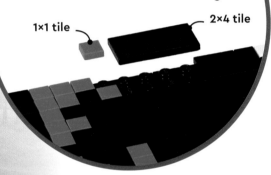

1×1 tile

2×4 tile

Top of the charts

The spacecraft *Voyager 1* and *Voyager 2* were sent into space in 1977. Scientists put a golden record on each one containing images and audio recordings of daily life, music, and people saying hello to give aliens an idea of life on Earth. The record also had pictures of humans and directions for how to find Earth.

Numbers 1 through 10

Information about DNA

A stick figure of a human

Map of the solar system

Drawing of the Arecibo telescope

Arecibo message

The Arecibo message was one of several radio messages that scientists sent into space with the hope that someday intelligent aliens might receive one and respond to it! It includes information about humans and Earth's place in the solar system.

WOW!
The Arecibo message was sent toward a cluster of stars known as M13, which is about **21,000** light-years away.

YOU CAN PLAY MUSIC WITH THIS THING?

IMAGINE!
What might **aliens** want to tell us on Earth? Build a message with images.

What shape is our galaxy?

Our galaxy is called the Milky Way. From Earth, it looks like a beautiful fuzzy streak of stars across the sky. But if we could see it from space, it would look like a bright disk with two main arms spiraling out from a bright center. The Milky Way is made of hundreds of billions of stars, huge clouds of gas and dust, and billions of planets.

Not all the stars in the Milky Way travel at the same speed

Did you know?

LEGO® Icons Galaxy Explorer (set 10497) is a modern reimagining of a LEGO® Space set from 1979. It has room for four minifigure astronauts in the front and a moon buggy and a robot in the back.

All shapes and sizes

Galaxies are huge collections of stars held together by gravity. All the stars orbit around the center in the same way planets orbit around their stars. Some galaxies, like the Milky Way, are spiral-shaped. Others, called elliptical galaxies, are ball-shaped. Galaxies with shapes that aren't spiral or elliptical are called irregular.

When galaxies collide

The biggest galaxy near the Milky Way is called the Andromeda Galaxy. Andromeda and the Milky Way are being pulled toward each other. In about four billion years, they will merge into an even bigger galaxy!

WOW!
The Milky Way is so big it takes light **100,000 years** to go from one side to the other.

A star is born

New stars form in parts of galaxies called stellar nurseries. Stellar nurseries contain lots of gas and dust left over from previous stars, and are mostly found in the spiral arms.

REALLY!
There are **hundreds of billions** of galaxies in the observable universe!

LOOKS LIKE THINGS ARE SPIRALING OUT OF CONTROL!

BUILD IT!

This mosaic is made from nine sections that connect in just a few places, making it easy to move in stages. Each section is a 16-stud square with three or four overhanging plates.

Overhanging plates connect the sections

89

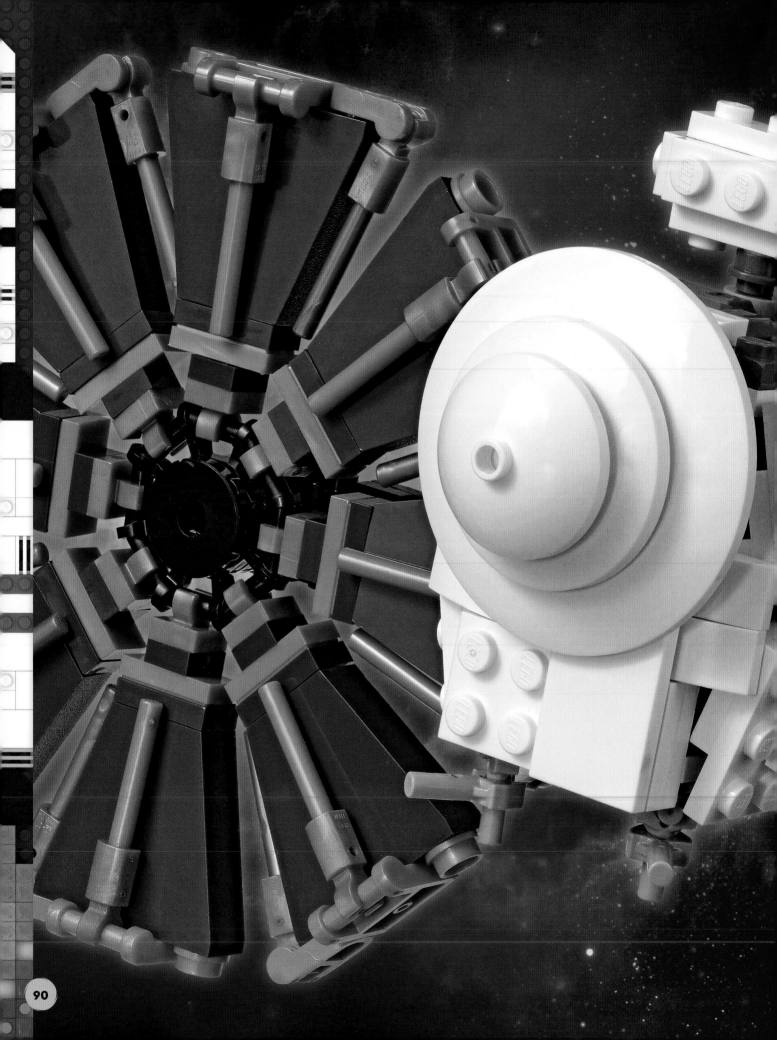

Exploring Space

Every year more missions blast off to explore new corners of the universe. Rovers roll across Martian deserts and giant telescopes peer back to the early days of galaxy formation. Humanity's knowledge grows as new technologies help us reach farther and see more clearly than ever before. But there is still plenty left to uncover.

Where does space begin?

Above our heads are many miles of air. The air around us is called the atmosphere. It is held to Earth by gravity. The higher up you go, the thinner the atmosphere becomes. There is no clear boundary between Earth's atmosphere and the start of space. Earth's atmosphere is divided into five layers. We live in the bottom layer, called the troposphere.

REALLY!
A thin layer of **ozone** in the stratosphere helps protect us from space radiation.

Karman line

The Karman line is sometimes considered the official start of space. It is 62 miles (100 km) above sea level. Any craft that flies above the Karman line is considered a spacecraft.

Low Earth orbit ends around here

Exobase

Karman line—low Earth orbit begins above here

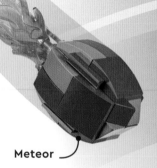

Meteor

Ozone

LIGHTS, CAMERA, ACTION!

Light display

Auroras are beautiful displays of light in the sky that happen when particles from the sun hit our atmosphere and cause it to glow. Auroras are sometimes called the northern lights or the southern lights because they are usually seen close to the north or south poles.

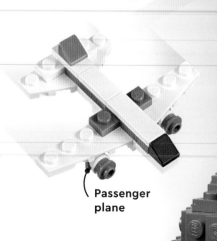

Passenger plane

Rocket

Exosphere

WOW!
Planets aren't the only thing with atmospheres; **the sun** has one, too!

Did you know?

LEGO® Ideas International Space Station (set 21321) is the second LEGO® version of the ISS. This one comes with two astronaut microfigures and a microscale Space Shuttle.

Thermosphere

Space station is in low Earth orbit

Low Earth orbit

Satellites that orbit very close to Earth—between about 100 and 1,200 miles (160 and 2,000 km)—are in a region around the planet called low Earth orbit, or LEO. LEO is so close to Earth that the satellites are in the thermosphere and still rub up against little bits of air.

Mesosphere

Jet

Stratosphere

BUILD IT!

This balloon build is designed to look round from the front or back, but flat from the sides. It's a great technique for making picturelike displays, intended to be seen from just one angle.

1×1 brick with four side studs

4×4 radar dish

1×1 plate with bar

Skeleton arm

Troposphere

Hot-air balloon

MIGHT NEED TO UPGRADE MY VEHICLE...

What were the first missions to space?

The first successful spacecraft launched into orbit was a satellite called Sputnik 1. Sputnik 1 was launched by the Soviet Union on October 4, 1957, and remained operational for three weeks. Sputnik 1's launch marks the beginning of the Space Age, when space exploration and technology developed.

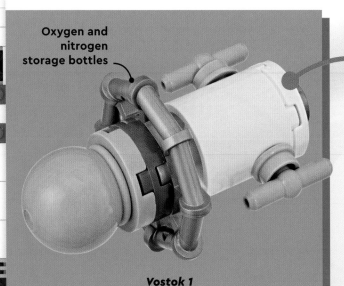

Oxygen and nitrogen storage bottles

Vostok 1

Destination: space

The first human to go into space was Russian cosmonaut Yuri Gagarin on April 12, 1961, in the *Vostok 1* spacecraft. The first American astronaut, Alan Shepard, launched a month later.

BUILD IT!

This model is made almost entirely from round pieces! The spherical cabin is a globe piece, and the rear is a round brick more often used to make droids.

Plate with ring of bars

LEGO® Technic axle

1×1 round plate with open stud

HEY! WAIT FOR ME!

Destination: the moon

Apollo 11 was the first mission to land humans on a celestial body other than Earth. On July 20, 1969, Neil Armstrong and Buzz Aldrin walked on the moon. They took pictures and brought back moon rocks for scientists to study.

Aluminum sphere measured 1 foot 11 inches (58 cm) across

WOW!
The first animals sent into space were **fruit flies** in February 1947!

Sputnik 1

Radio antennas sent signals to Earth

Did you know?

The first astronauts on the LEGO moon were the brick-built figures in **Space Module with Astronauts (set 367)**. The set was released in 1975—just six years after the first real-life moon landing!

Destination: the sun

The *Parker Solar Probe* is the first spacecraft ever to touch the sun! On April 28, 2021, the uncrewed craft flew through the corona, or upper atmosphere of the sun and took samples of it.

How are rockets launched?

We use rockets to overcome Earth's very strong gravity. To get all the way into orbit, a rocket has to be lifted up faster than gravity can pull it back down. Rockets do this by burning fuel and letting the exhaust from the explosion escape from the back of the rocket. This creates a push called thrust.

Up and away!

Thrust can lift a rocket up because of a law in physics figured out by scientist Isaac Newton in the 17th century. Newton's third law of motion states that for every action there is an equal and opposite reaction. When the rocket blasts exhaust out the bottom, it has to move in the opposite direction—UP!

I MUST STOP WALKING NEAR APPLE TREES!

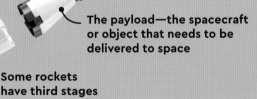

The payload—the spacecraft or object that needs to be delivered to space

Some rockets have third stages

Second stage

The first stage is the first one to run out of fuel

Reusable stages

It takes a lot of fuel to lift a rocket into orbit! Fuel can be heavy, so rockets usually split into parts called stages. Each stage carries fuel. When the fuel gets used up, the stage drops away, to stop it from weighing down the rest of the rocket. Some new rockets are being designed with reusable first stages so that an entirely new rocket doesn't need to be built every time one is launched.

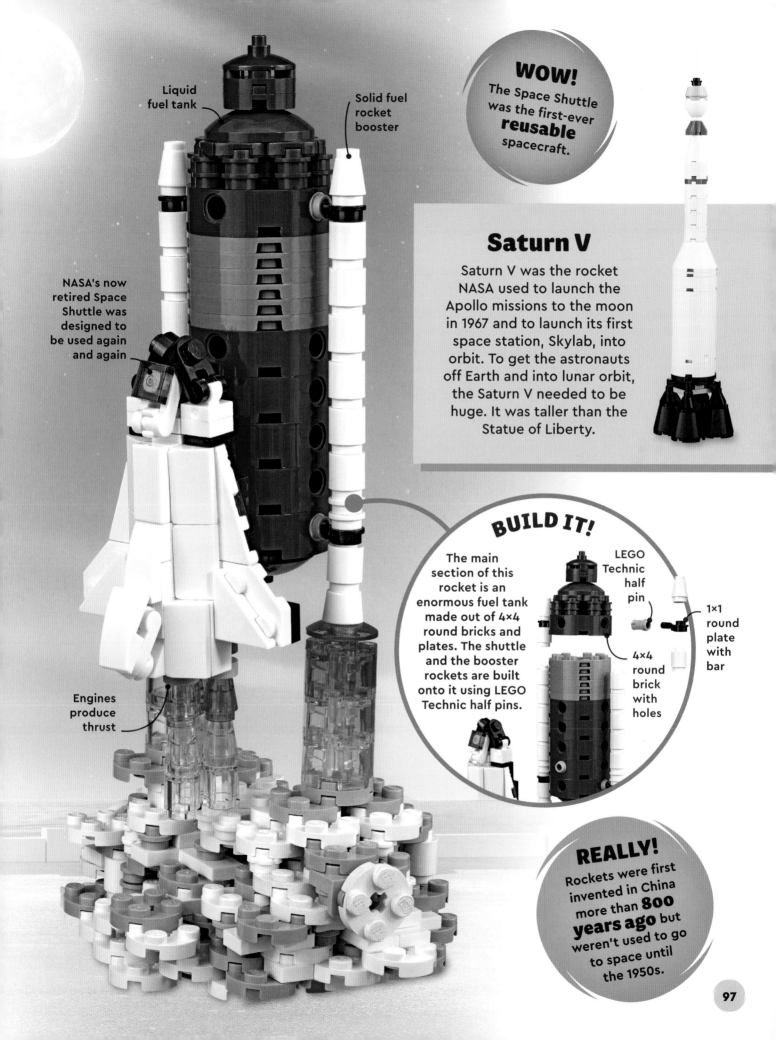

Liquid fuel tank

Solid fuel rocket booster

NASA's now retired Space Shuttle was designed to be used again and again

Engines produce thrust

WOW!
The Space Shuttle was the first-ever **reusable** spacecraft.

Saturn V

Saturn V was the rocket NASA used to launch the Apollo missions to the moon in 1967 and to launch its first space station, Skylab, into orbit. To get the astronauts off Earth and into lunar orbit, the Saturn V needed to be huge. It was taller than the Statue of Liberty.

BUILD IT!

The main section of this rocket is an enormous fuel tank made out of 4×4 round bricks and plates. The shuttle and the booster rockets are built onto it using LEGO Technic half pins.

LEGO Technic half pin

1×1 round plate with bar

4×4 round brick with holes

REALLY!
Rockets were first invented in China more than **800 years ago** but weren't used to go to space until the 1950s.

How do spacecraft get their power?

Just like machines on Earth, spacecraft need electricity to run their computers and equipment. But they can't just plug into the wall when their power gets low. So, engineers have to design ways for them to recharge their batteries wherever they are in space. Most craft, like the *Lucy* spacecraft that is studying asteroids, use solar panels, but a few use small nuclear power generators to create electricity.

Each panel is about 24 feet (7 m) wide

Power up!

Electricity is a type of energy made from electrons (tiny particles) moving through materials. Electricity can be converted into other useful forms of energy like heat, movement, or light.

Lucy's solar panels look like giant fans

WOW!
The International Space Station's solar panel array would cover almost half a **soccer pitch!**

Did you know?

Plant leaves and flowers are nature's original solar panels, converting light into energy. **LEGO® Icons Wildflower Bouquet (set 10313)** includes eight species with different sun-catching shapes.

Solar energy

Spacecraft in the solar system capture energy from the sun using solar panels similar to the ones you might see on a building. The bigger the panels, the more power they can generate.

Far, far away

Some spacecraft are too far away from the sun to use solar panels, because solar panels need bright light to work. Instead, these craft use small amounts of radioactive material, such as plutonium. Warmth from this material can power devices called radioisotope thermoelectric generators (RTGs) to create electricity.

Cameras for studying asteroids

BUILD IT!

Upside-down 1×2 plate with bar

Upside-down 1×1 plate with bar

Upside-down 1×2×3 slope

Upside-down 1×1 tile with clip

Plate with ring of bars

This flowerlike solar array is made from eight identical sections fanning out from a plate with ring of bars. Both arrays are supported by bars attached to the base of the model.

THESE SOLAR PANELS REALLY BRIGHTEN MY DAY!

REALLY!
The element **plutonium** is named after **Pluto**.

What is mission control?

Space missions need help from people back on Earth. Mission control is the group of scientists and engineers that help astronauts or robots in space know where to go or what to do in an emergency. The mission control team have lots of computers they use to stay up to date about all the important information they need to make decisions.

Did you know?

When Olivia and her friends go into space in **LEGO® Friends Olivia's Space Academy (set 41713)**, mission control is on the top floor. The building also includes a classroom and an observatory.

Take control

Ground-based mission control monitors and controls space flights, and in modern spacecraft much of the control is automated. This allows astronauts to focus on other things like performing science experiments. But if astronauts need to, they can manually pilot their spacecraft using the capsule's controls.

Quick change

Once in space, a spacecraft will keep moving in the direction it is already going. To change direction in space, it has small rockets called thrusters that it can fire.

Piloting astronauts use a variety of screens, switches, and controls

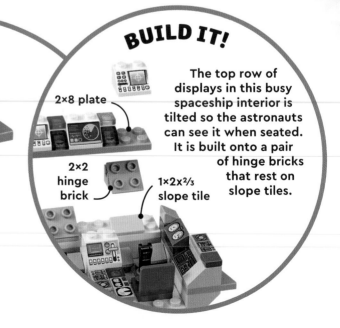

BUILD IT!

The top row of displays in this busy spaceship interior is tilted so the astronauts can see it when seated. It is built onto a pair of hinge bricks that rest on slope tiles.

2×8 plate

2×2 hinge brick

1×2×2/3 slope tile

REALLY!
The flight director is the **leader** of the mission control team. They make the final call in an emergency.

Large screens make data visible to all

Capsule communicators (CAPCOMs) liaise with the astronauts

I'M DOING A COFFEE RUN. ANYONE FOR A LATTE?

Data is used to make decisions on next steps for the mission

Deep Space Network

When spacecraft are far away from Earth, it can be hard to communicate with them. The Deep Space Network (DSN) is made of giant radio dishes all over the globe so that no matter where a craft is, there will always be a dish pointed in its direction.

WOW!
The Deep Space Network received the **first footage** of humans walking on the moon in 1969.

How does a space suit work?

Outer space is very different from Earth, so astronauts need suits to provide the conditions their bodies are used to on Earth. Space suits supply air for them to breathe and the correct temperature and pressure. Astronauts need space suits any time they leave their spaceship to work in space.

Did you know?

LEGO® Creator Space Astronaut (set 31152) is a 647-piece posable model of a scientist on a space walk. It can be rebuilt as a futuristic spacecraft, or as a dog in a space suit with four legs and a tail!

To the extreme

Space suits must be able to protect astronauts from both extreme cold and heat. Objects facing the sun, like the day side of the moon, can heat up to hundreds of degrees. Objects in shadow, like the night side of the moon, can drop to hundreds of degrees below freezing.

THIS TANK GIVES ME BREATHING ROOM.

Oxygen tanks are essential gear

Take a breath

Humans and other animals need air to breathe. There are lots of different kinds of gases in the air. Oxygen is a particularly important gas we can't live without! Astronauts need to bring oxygen with them to breathe.

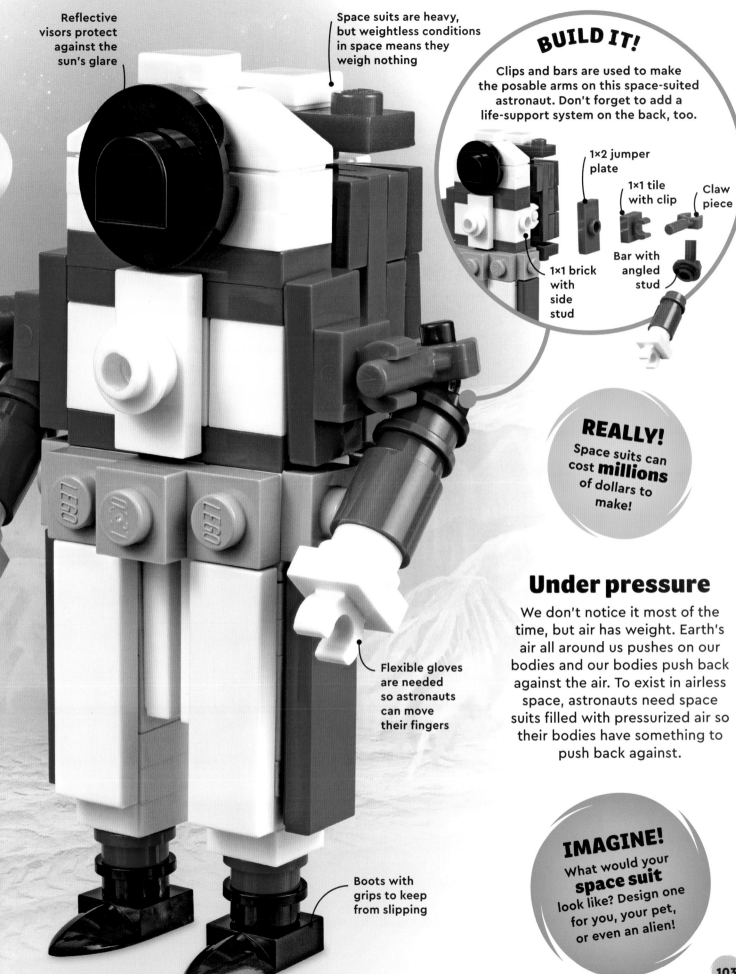

Reflective visors protect against the sun's glare

Space suits are heavy, but weightless conditions in space means they weigh nothing

BUILD IT!

Clips and bars are used to make the posable arms on this space-suited astronaut. Don't forget to add a life-support system on the back, too.

1×2 jumper plate

1×1 tile with clip

Claw piece

1×1 brick with side stud

Bar with angled stud

REALLY!

Space suits can cost **millions** of dollars to make!

Flexible gloves are needed so astronauts can move their fingers

Under pressure

We don't notice it most of the time, but air has weight. Earth's air all around us pushes on our bodies and our bodies push back against the air. To exist in airless space, astronauts need space suits filled with pressurized air so their bodies have something to push back against.

Boots with grips to keep from slipping

IMAGINE!

What would your **space suit** look like? Design one for you, your pet, or even an alien!

How did humans land on the moon?

BUILD IT!

You don't need lots of pieces to create an awesome model. This microscale Lunar Module is made from just 11 pieces.

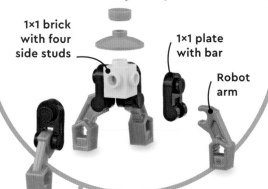

1×1 brick with four side studs

1×1 plate with bar

Robot arm

In the 1960s and 1970s, NASA's Apollo program landed 12 astronauts on the moon. The first person to set foot on the moon was American astronaut Neil Armstrong on July 20, 1969, on a lunar plain called the Sea of Tranquility. Each mission launched astronauts from Earth in Saturn V rockets and landed them on the moon in lunar landers. They brought lots of cool tech to help them explore. Three missions even brought buggies to drive around in.

Did you know?

LEGO® Creator Expert NASA Apollo 11 Lunar Lander (set 10266) is a detailed re-creation of the first crewed vessel to land on the moon. It includes minifigure astronauts and a brick-built lunar surface.

Lunar Module

Each mission had a lunar lander spacecraft called the Lunar Module that carried humans to the moon and launched them back off it. It was launched on the Saturn V rocket along with the astronauts from Earth.

Coming home

Returning to Earth is one of the trickiest parts of space flight. As the spacecraft plunges through the atmosphere it rubs up against the air and becomes hot from the friction, just like a shooting star! Engineers have to make sure the craft can slow down and not burn up before it hits the ground.

Radio dish and antenna to send TV signals to Earth

LET'S GO FOR A SPIN!

Gravity on the moon

The moon's gravity is lower than Earth's because it is so much smaller. This lets astronauts jump much higher than they could on Earth and to float around in space!

REALLY!
There were only **66 years** between the first airplane flight and the first moon landing!

HOLD ON TIGHT—IT'S A BUMPY RIDE!

WOW!
Apollo astronauts brought back **842 pounds** (382 kg) of moon rocks.

Color TV camera filmed the Lunar Module's liftoff from the moon

Two large batteries powered the buggy

Tires made of woven steel wire for improved grip

105

How do people live in space?

Astronauts live in space on space stations, which are specially designed satellites that orbit around Earth. The astronauts keep busy by making sure everything in the space station works and by performing many experiments. The stations have to provide everything a human needs to survive, such as the right temperatures; air to breathe; and places to sleep, eat, and exercise.

Did you know?

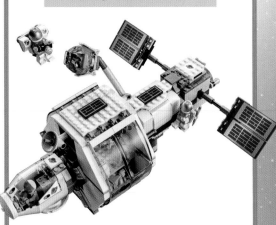

LEGO® City Lunar Space Station (set 60349) is inspired by NASA's plans to build a space station in orbit around the moon.

REALLY!
The first space station was **Salyut 1**, launched by the Soviet Union in 1971.

Space food

Food from Earth needs to be launched into space for astronauts to eat. It is not safe to have open flames to cook food, so meals must be eaten cold or heated in a microwave.

I THOUGHT YOU SAID DEEP DISH, NOT DEEP SPACE...

BUILD IT!

This space station build has larger round bricks at one end than the other. In the middle, bricks with side studs provide connection points for the two solar panel assemblies.

Sideways 1×2 brick with side stud

Bar

1×2 plate with clip

Solar panels power the space station

JUST POPPING OUT FOR A STROLL!

Space walks

Sometimes astronauts need to work outside of their spacecraft. They wear protective space suits with oxygen tanks so they can breathe, and use a tether to make sure they don't float away.

Solar panels are steerable

WOW!
The **International Space Station** (ISS) is about as long as a football field.

Docking

When astronauts launch from Earth, their vehicle needs to connect to the space station. This is called docking. Once the two craft are safely locked together, astronauts go back and forth between the two.

Space ferry docks with the space station

How does space exploration help us on Earth?

Humans love to explore for the sake of adventure and the pursuit of knowledge! But exploring space has a lot of practical applications, too. Space helps us learn about and take better care of Earth. Satellites in orbit around Earth can help us monitor our planet and communicate with each other over vast distances.

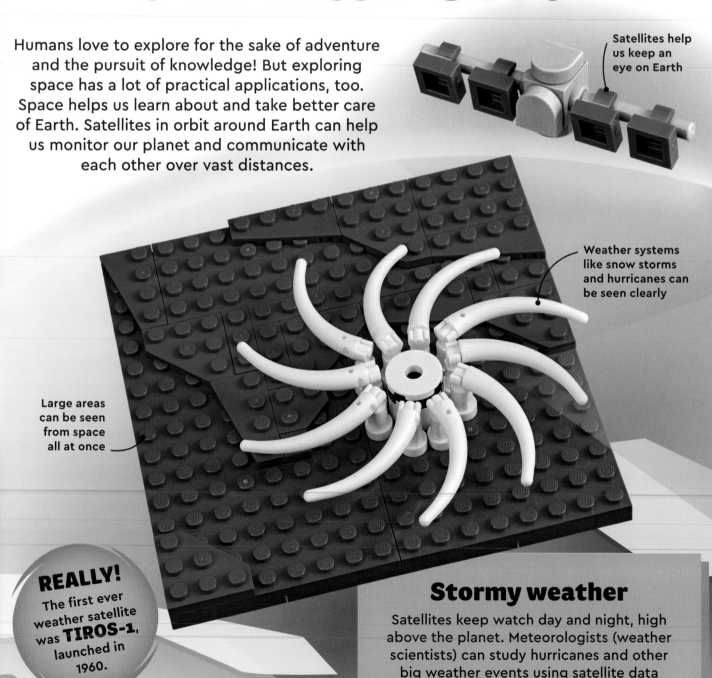

Satellites help us keep an eye on Earth

Weather systems like snow storms and hurricanes can be seen clearly

Large areas can be seen from space all at once

Stormy weather

Satellites keep watch day and night, high above the planet. Meteorologists (weather scientists) can study hurricanes and other big weather events using satellite data and help people down on Earth stay safe.

Phone home

Satellites can provide mobile phone and internet service to rural (or countryside), areas on Earth that would not have access. There are thousands of communication satellites orbiting Earth right now.

Did you know?

NASA's research into shock absorption helps make the latest artificial limbs. The first LEGO City minifigure to have a modern artificial limb is a customer in **LEGO® City Grocery Store (set 60347).**

BUILD IT!

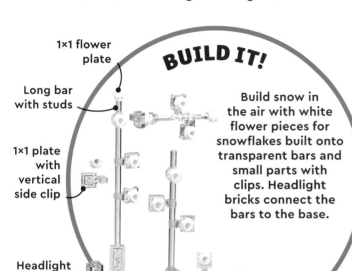

1×1 flower plate

Long bar with studs

1×1 plate with vertical side clip

Headlight brick

Build snow in the air with white flower pieces for snowflakes built onto transparent bars and small parts with clips. Headlight bricks connect the bars to the base.

HAVE YOU TRIED TURNING IT OFF AND ON AGAIN?

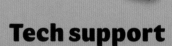

Tech support

Many useful technologies that we use every day were invented to help in space exploration. Some examples include fitness monitors, infrared thermometers, and even laptops!

THIS WEATHER'S SNOW JOKE!

Scientists use data from both Earth and space to better understand the planet

WOW!
The first **wireless headsets** were invented for astronauts to communicate on the moon.

109

What is space junk?

Dead satellites and broken pieces of spacecraft are called space junk. Space junk is debris left over from previous missions, and there is lots of it in orbit around Earth. It can be dangerous if craft cross paths with junk, or if the junk falls back to Earth and hits something.

Discarded rocket booster

Graveyard shift

Sometimes when satellite missions are over, the satellite is pushed into a higher orbit full of other "dead" satellites, called a graveyard orbit. The satellites in graveyard orbits will eventually fall back to Earth, but not for hundreds of years.

WOW!
Most space junk **burns up** like a meteor before it hits the ground.

Crash landing

Skylab was NASA's first space station. In 1979, it crashed back to Earth after its mission was over. No one was hurt, but pieces of it did fall in areas of Australia where a lot of people lived. The event inspired planners to be more careful about what happens to spacecraft when missions are complete so that pieces burn up before they get to Earth.

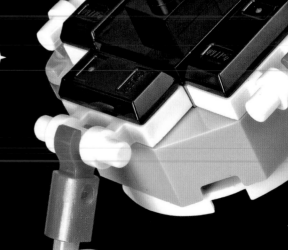

Old satellite left in orbit

AND THEY SAY JUNK FOOD IS BAD FOR YOU...

REALLY!

There are more than **26,500** known pieces of space junk.

Cleaning up

Engineers and scientists are working on ways to clean up space junk. We can use telescopes to locate and track the junk. Then we could use giant nets attached to spacecraft to collect it, or even shoot the trash with lasers so it safely burns up in the atmosphere.

Into the Future

Our adventure has only just begun! What does the future of space exploration hold? Will humans transform whole planets and build massive space stations? Will we travel to distant stars or discover the nature of the universe itself? Maybe we will invent something we could have never even dreamed of. Let's find out!

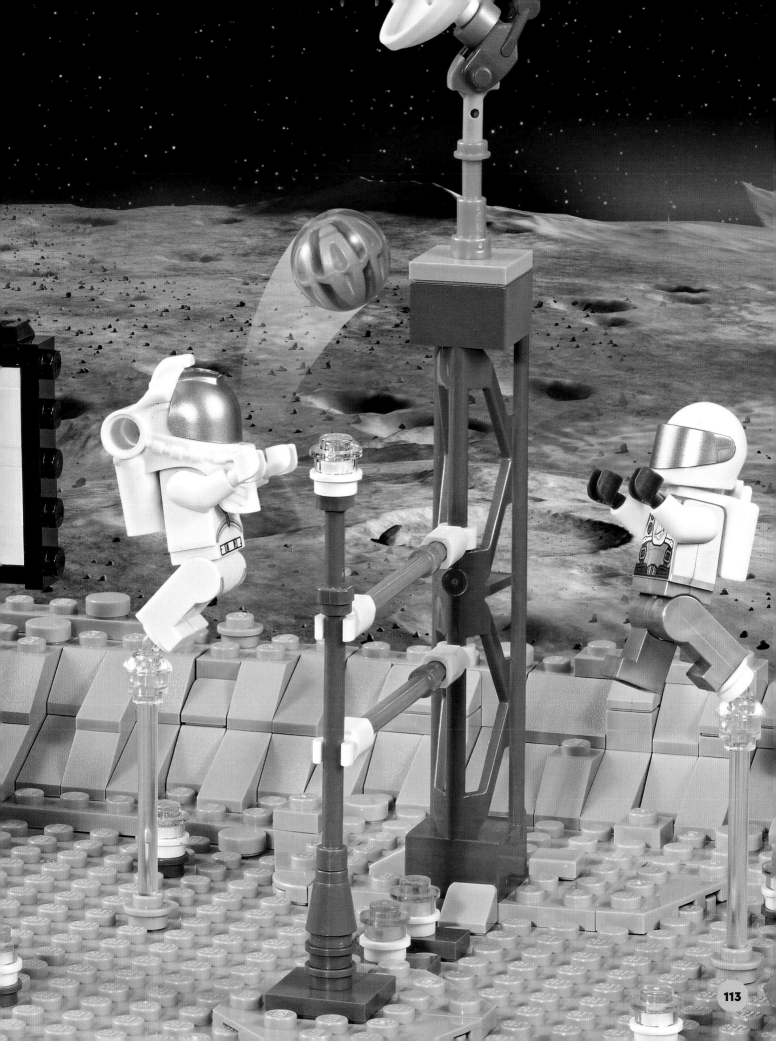

Could you go on a space vacation?

One day soon, space tourism may be more widely available! Imagine taking a cruise around the moon, playing in microgravity, or peering back at beautiful blue Earth from high above the atmosphere! What do you think it would be like to play basketball or volleyball in the moon's low gravity?

Flying fairly high

Suborbital flights are available today through private space companies like Blue Origin and Virgin Galactic. On a suborbital flight, passengers go up into space, far above most of the atmosphere, but they don't go all the way around the planet. They come back down after a few minutes in space.

Did you know?

A school trip to space sounds like a dream, making it the perfect mission for Dream Chasers Logan, Mateo, and Mr. Oz in **LEGO® DREAMZzz™ Mr. Oz's Spacebus (set 71460)!**

21 POINTS VS. 19!

Robots will help humans with everyday jobs

CHECK OUT THIS SPIKE!

REALLY!
The first space tourist visited the **ISS** in 2001.

Tourists will need air tanks to breathe

Room with a view

A space hotel would be a space station where guests could stay as they orbited Earth. Most satellites would travel in low Earth orbit (LEO), the region of space closest to Earth. It only takes a satellite in LEO about 90 minutes to go around the planet once, so guests would get to see 16 sunrises and sunsets a day.

OUR FINEST ROCKET DOG, SIR!

Into the future

One day, people may be able to visit more distant worlds of our solar system like Mars or Venus, or Vesta in the asteroid belt. Engineers and scientists are working hard to create new opportunities and open the way to space.

Space tourists will use radio to communicate with Earth

BUILD IT!

This robo-butler is built around a brick with side studs. Its lower body is a telescope piece on a small radar dish, and its face is a printed 1×1 round tile on a 1×1 bracket plate.

1×1 brick with four side studs

Claw piece

1×1 round plate with a bar

I WILL... WHEN IT GETS HERE.

WOW! The youngest person to visit space was **18 years old.**

What would a colony on the moon look like?

A permanent base on the moon would be a great base for exploring our satellite and going farther into space. People would have to live inside special buildings designed to protect them from the low pressure, high radiation, and big swings in temperature that happen on the lunar surface. Colonists might live inside interconnected big domes or deep inside tunnels.

Location, location

Planners would want to locate the colony somewhere there were lots of resources for mining. They would have to find suitable natural features to build in, such as craters or tunnels left by flowing lava.

Solar panels will generate electricity

NICE (LAUNCH) PAD!

BUILD IT!

The sides of this moon buggy are built on using bars and clips. The driver's control column is built around a minifigure blaster with four studs, and slots into a 1×2 jumper plate.

Sideways 1×2 plate with bar

Minifigure blaster with four studs

1×2 jumper plate

1×2 plate with clips

Moon buggies are great for getting around!

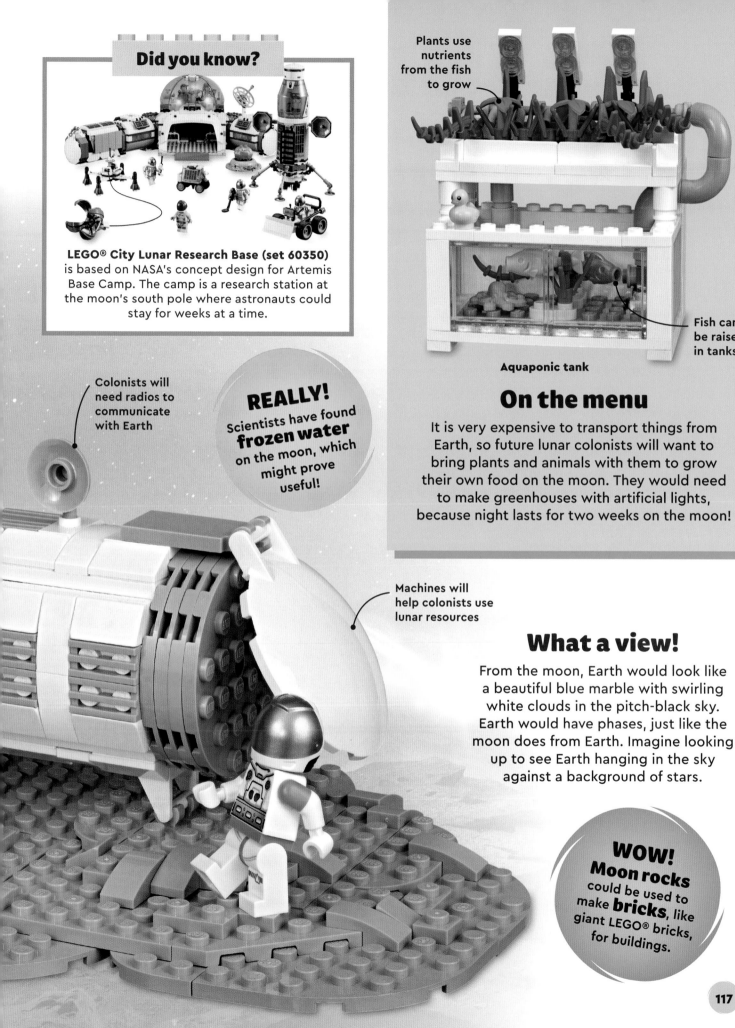

Plants use nutrients from the fish to grow

Fish can be raised in tanks

Aquaponic tank

On the menu

It is very expensive to transport things from Earth, so future lunar colonists will want to bring plants and animals with them to grow their own food on the moon. They would need to make greenhouses with artificial lights, because night lasts for two weeks on the moon!

Colonists will need radios to communicate with Earth

REALLY!
Scientists have found **frozen water** on the moon, which might prove useful!

Machines will help colonists use lunar resources

What a view!

From the moon, Earth would look like a beautiful blue marble with swirling white clouds in the pitch-black sky. Earth would have phases, just like the moon does from Earth. Imagine looking up to see Earth hanging in the sky against a background of stars.

WOW!
Moon rocks could be used to make **bricks**, like giant LEGO® bricks, for buildings.

117

Could humans live on huge space stations?

In the future, humans could build giant cities orbiting around planets or maybe even around objects like black holes! These cities would need to produce their own power and grow food. They would require places for spaceships to dock and a way to communicate with other stations. Some planets could have lots of stations orbiting around them or maybe just one big station.

Views out the window would be amazing!

Did you know?

The eight sections of the giant **LEGO® City Modular Space Station (set 60433)** can be broken away from the center ring and rearranged. You can even make a kind of space train!

WOW!
It took more than **40 missions** to put the International Space Station together.

BUILD IT!

The portals dividing each section of this space station are made from sideways half-arch pieces. The ones at the top are back to back and only connected by clips attached to a bar.

Sideways 1×1 plate with clip

Bar

Sideways 1×5×4 half-arch

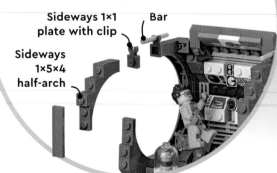

Brick by brick

Space stations would be too big to build on Earth and launch into space in one piece. Instead, stations could be built in smaller pieces and assembled in space, just like smaller stations such as the International Space Station.

Space station jobs

There would be lots of important jobs to be filled to make a space station functional. The station would need engineers and builders to keep it going, but it would also need farmers to grow food and teachers and librarians to educate people. It would need scientists and adventurers to explore and learn more about space, too!

Space hotels could house space tourists and space station staff

People would need special places to sleep and eat

Tubes would carry air around the station

DON'T MIND ME—I'M JUST DRIFTING OFF...

IMAGINE! What would your **dream bedroom** look like in space? What cool things would it have? Build a cozy pod!

Go for a spin

Being in microgravity or zero-G for long periods of time isn't good for the human body. But large space stations could create artificial gravity by spinning. The faster the space station spins, the stronger the gravity will be.

REALLY! The current longest stay on a space station is **437 days**.

Could we make other planets more like Earth?

Changing a planet to be more like Earth is called terraforming. Many scientists are excited about the idea of terraforming Mars. Mars is very similar to Earth, so it might be easier to terraform than other planets. To terraform Mars, humans would need to thicken the atmosphere so that Mars could stay warmer. Once Mars warmed up, the water ice at its poles could melt and create oceans, rivers, and lakes.

> I TOLD YOU THIS WAS A GOOD PLACE FOR A VACATION!

WOW!
Mars's **day length** is almost the same as Earth's.

Mars's soil is red because it has iron in it

Keep cool

Venus is very hot compared to Earth because it has a thick atmosphere that traps heat. To terraform Venus, scientists would have to figure out how to cool down the planet. They might build a sun shield to block some of the light or carry away some of Venus's atmosphere into space on giant spaceships.

Asteroids

Other places to terraform might be the inside of asteroids! They could be hollowed out and made to spin. The spin could create artificial gravity, and the hollow asteroid could be filled with air, soil, water, and living things.

REALLY!
Giant mirrors in space could direct light to Mars and make it warmer.

Plants could make oxygen for people to breathe

Lunar changes

The moon is much closer to Earth than Mars or Venus. To terraform it, scientists would have to figure out how to create air around the moon, giving it an atmosphere that would let humans breathe.

Water could be a home for fish and plants

121

Could you ride an elevator into space?

Currently, getting into space is expensive! It takes lots of fuel to lift a rocket off the ground and all the way out of the atmosphere. If we invent less expensive ways to get into space, we could send out more missions—for research purposes and for fun! One idea would be to build a giant elevator connected to a satellite that lifts cargo (and people) all the way to space. Instead of blasting into space, you could just take an elevator ride!

REALLY!
It took almost **1,000,000 gallons** (3,800,000 liters) of fuel for Saturn V to get to the moon.

Elevator anchored at the equator

Did you know?

LEGO® Monkie Kid Galactic Explorer (set 80035) is perfect for when Monkie Kid wants to go on a mission into space. The rocket has room for Monkie Kid and four of his friends as well as a jet pack and a moon buggy.

Escape velocity

If you weren't being lifted up by a space elevator but wanted to get off Earth, you'd need to know your escape velocity. This is how fast you would have to be going to not get pulled back down by gravity.

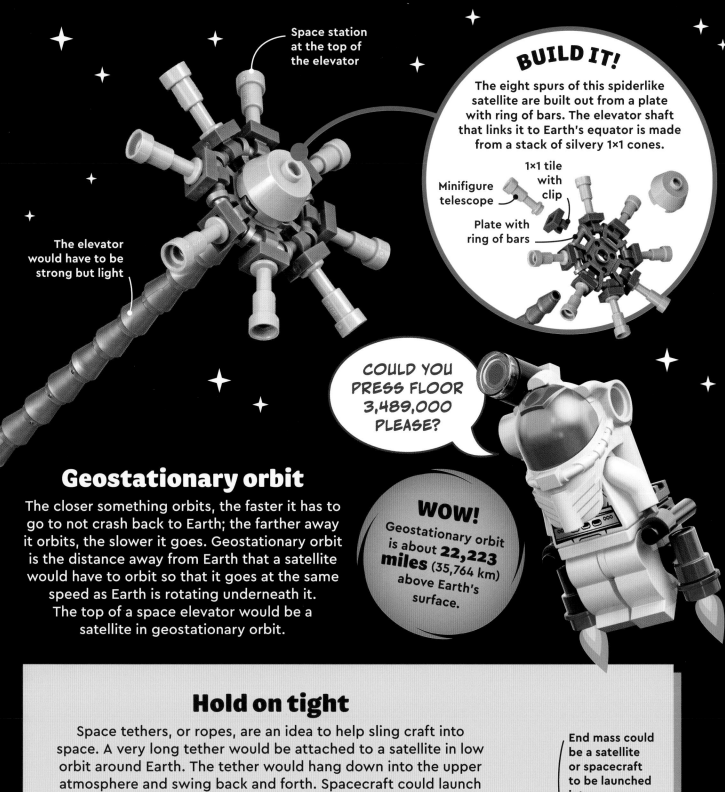

Space station at the top of the elevator

BUILD IT!

The eight spurs of this spiderlike satellite are built out from a plate with ring of bars. The elevator shaft that links it to Earth's equator is made from a stack of silvery 1×1 cones.

Minifigure telescope

1×1 tile with clip

Plate with ring of bars

The elevator would have to be strong but light

COULD YOU PRESS FLOOR 3,489,000 PLEASE?

Geostationary orbit

The closer something orbits, the faster it has to go to not crash back to Earth; the farther away it orbits, the slower it goes. Geostationary orbit is the distance away from Earth that a satellite would have to orbit so that it goes at the same speed as Earth is rotating underneath it. The top of a space elevator would be a satellite in geostationary orbit.

WOW!
Geostationary orbit is about **22,223 miles** (35,764 km) above Earth's surface.

Hold on tight

Space tethers, or ropes, are an idea to help sling craft into space. A very long tether would be attached to a satellite in low orbit around Earth. The tether would hang down into the upper atmosphere and swing back and forth. Spacecraft could launch and hook onto the tether to get tossed into space.

End mass could be a satellite or spacecraft to be launched into space

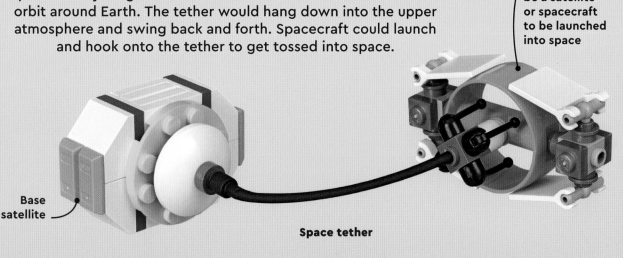

Base satellite

Space tether

How will we reach other stars and planets?

Stars are light-years apart from each other. To reach other stars and their planets, we will have to develop advanced forms of space flight. Even traveling close to the speed of light, it will take many years to reach other stars. Space travelers of the future will need to bring everything they will need with them.

REALLY!
If space probe *Voyager 1* were headed toward the closest star to the sun, it would take more than **70,000 years** to get there!

BUILD IT!

Rollercoaster track piece

The artificial gravity ring of this futuristic spacecraft is made from four curved sections of rollercoaster track. Straight sections are used to scaffold the middle of the main hull.

2×4 plate

Spinning will help create artificial gravity

Human colonies

One day, humans might be able to build homes on other worlds across the galaxy. We will have to learn how to find planets that could be suitable to live on and how to get to them.

Did you know?

LEGO® City Interstellar Spaceship (set 60430) is designed for traveling the vast distances between stars. It must move faster than light if the pilot hopes to make a return trip!

Light sails

Light sails use light to propel a craft through space, similar to how sailboats use wind on Earth. Light sails can use light from stars or from lasers. Spacecraft will need huge sails to catch as much light as possible to reach other stars and their planets.

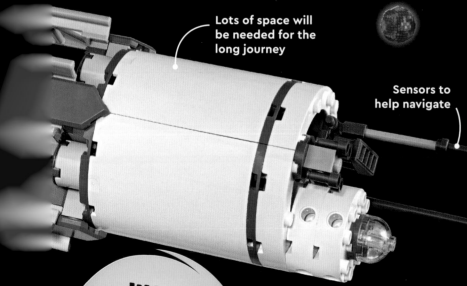

Lots of space will be needed for the long journey

Sensors to help navigate

ALMOST THERE. ONLY 14 MORE YEARS TO GO.

Ion thrusters

Ion thrusters are a good choice for long-distance space travel. They shoot tiny, charged particles out to push the spacecraft along. The engine can run for months, and, over time, ion thrusters can accelerate their craft to super fast speeds. They have been used on real missions such as *Dawn*, which visited the dwarf planet Ceres in 2015.

WOW!

The fastest spacecraft ever was the *Parker Solar Probe*, which went at **394,736 miles per hour** (635,266 kph) in 2023.

Could there be a multiverse?

Scientists have many ideas about the nature of our universe. To find out which ones are true, they need to find evidence or clues. One idea scientists want to find evidence for is the multiverse, which is the concept that there could be more universes than ours. So far we don't know, but we are still investigating.

Did you know?

Some LEGO sets seem to come from the multiverse! In 1979, US kids played with **LEGO® Space Galaxy Explorer (set 497)**, while in Europe the exact same set was called **Space Cruiser And Moonbase (set 928)**.

Inside black holes

Black hole cosmology is the idea that universes might be born inside black holes. If this is the case, every black hole might have a universe inside it containing billions of black holes of its own, each with another universe inside containing billions more black holes.

REALLY!
There may be as many as **100 million** black holes in our galaxy alone.

Our universe looks three-dimensional

DID I HEAR KNOCKING?

IMAGINE!
What might a **parallel universe** look like? Build an everyday scene on Earth... but with a few strange differences!

String it together

String theory is an attempt to solve the biggest questions about our universe at an incredibly small scale. This theory suggests that the smallest particles that make up everything around us are tiny vibrating strings. String theorists believe studying the effects of the vibrating strings would explain more about our universe.

WOW!
Parallel universe theory explores the possibility that there might be nearby universes that are almost **complete copies** of our own.

The holographic universe

Some scientists think our three-dimensional universe might actually be a special image called a hologram. This wouldn't mean that we aren't real; just that what we experience as three-dimensional comes from something that only has two dimensions.

IS THE HOLOGRAM REAL? AM I REAL?!

Could we travel between universes?

BUILD IT!

Vine piece

1×1 tile with clip

1×1 brick with four side studs

Make a pair of parallel worlds by building two almost mirror-image scenes with distinct differences. Here, one reality is black and white and inhabited by minifigure wolves!

Maybe some universes only have black-and-white landscapes

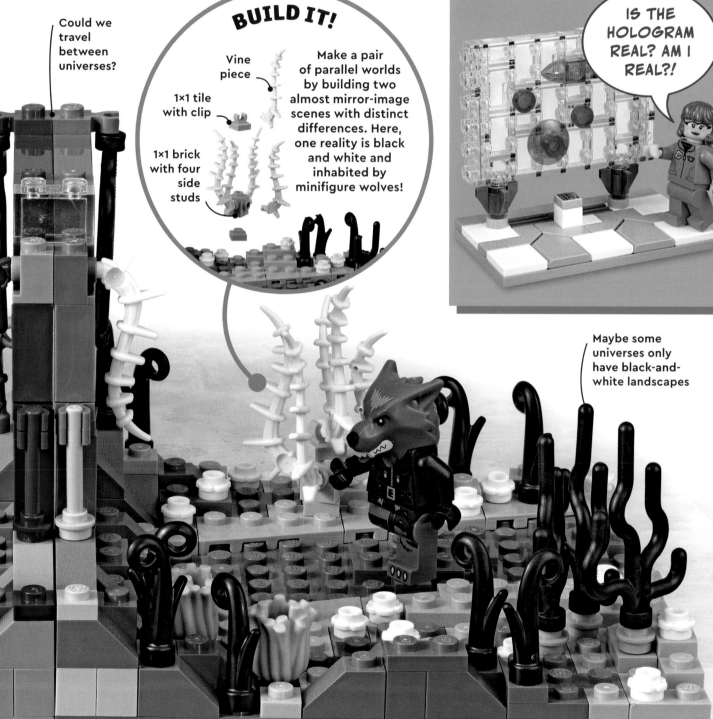

True or false?

There are a lot of amazing things that have happened in space!
Can you tell which of these facts are true and which ones are false?

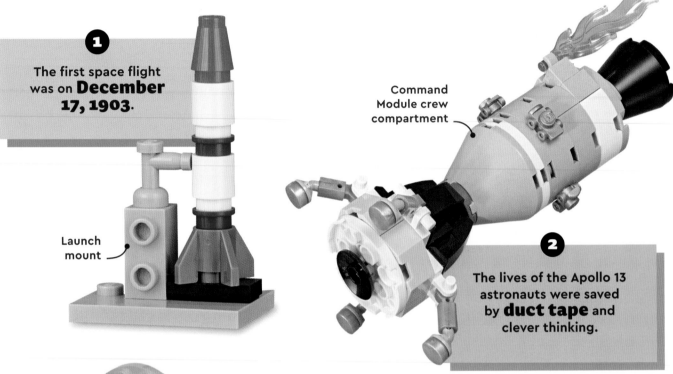

1
The first space flight was on **December 17, 1903**.

Launch mount

Command Module crew compartment

2
The lives of the Apollo 13 astronauts were saved by **duct tape** and clever thinking.

The sun's circumference is 2.7 million miles (4.4 million km)

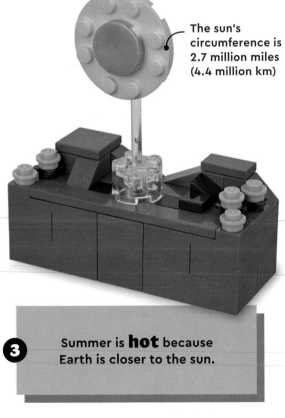

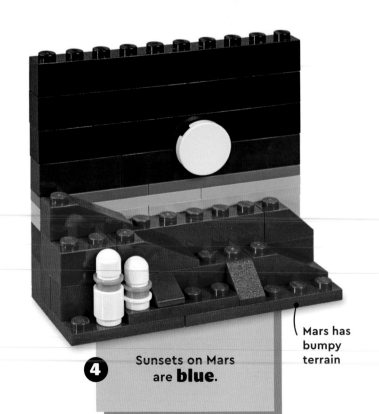

3
Summer is **hot** because Earth is closer to the sun.

Mars has bumpy terrain

4
Sunsets on Mars are **blue**.

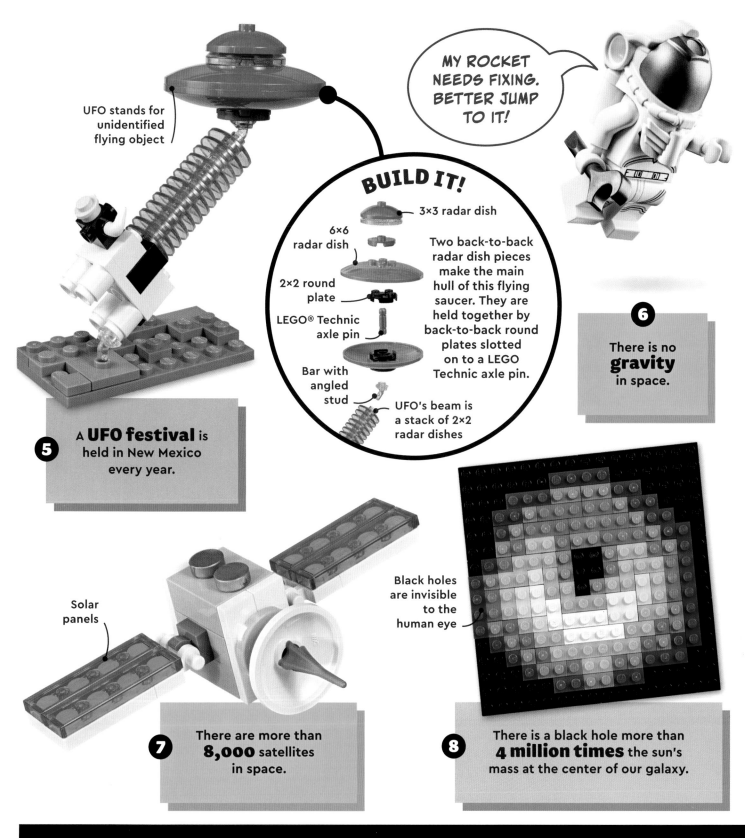

UFO stands for unidentified flying object

MY ROCKET NEEDS FIXING. BETTER JUMP TO IT!

BUILD IT!

3×3 radar dish

6×6 radar dish

2×2 round plate

LEGO® Technic axle pin

Bar with angled stud

Two back-to-back radar dish pieces make the main hull of this flying saucer. They are held together by back-to-back round plates slotted on to a LEGO Technic axle pin.

UFO's beam is a stack of 2×2 radar dishes

6 There is no **gravity** in space.

5 A **UFO festival** is held in New Mexico every year.

Solar panels

Black holes are invisible to the human eye

7 There are more than **8,000** satellites in space.

8 There is a black hole more than **4 million times** the sun's mass at the center of our galaxy.

---

1. False—December 17, 1903, is the date of the first flight on Earth by the Wright brothers. It wasn't until 1961 that the first human flew in space. **2. True**—After an oxygen tank exploded and carbon dioxide levels started to rise, the astronauts used duct tape and clever thinking to repair the filter system and survive. **3. False**—Seasons happen because Earth is tilted. When it is summer where you live, the part of Earth you are on is tilted toward the sun. In the winter, it is tilted away. **4. True**—At sunrise and sunset the light has to travel through more atmosphere than at midday when the sun is directly above Mars. The light is scattered through the extra atmosphere, making it look bluish. **5. True**—The festival takes place in Roswell, New Mexico, every summer. The town is famous for an alleged UFO crash in 1947. **6. False**—There is gravity everywhere! When astronauts are in orbit it looks like there is no gravity because they are in free fall around Earth (which looks like floating). They are experiencing most of Earth's gravity, but with nothing to stop them. **7. True**—There are thousands of satellites around Earth, and each year more are launched. **8. True**—The black hole at the center of our galaxy is a super massive black hole called Sagittarius A*. It is 4.3 million times more massive than our sun!

Build basics

The best thing about building with LEGO® bricks is that you can be creative and build in any way you like. It can be helpful to follow some basics, though, especially if you'd like to take on bigger or more complex models. Here are some tips to help you with your LEGO building.

Sort it!

Why not sort some of your bricks by type or color before you begin? This will save you time searching for bricks when building.

Do some research

Use the models in this book as inspiration or look online or in books for pictures of what you would like to build. You could even draw some rough sketches to help you plan your build.

Our Space Neighbors

Be creative

If you are copying a model in this book, you don't have to have the exact same pieces. Be inspired by these models to create your own amazing builds. If you don't have the perfect piece for a particular feature, find a creative solution. There's bound to be another piece that can create a similar effect.

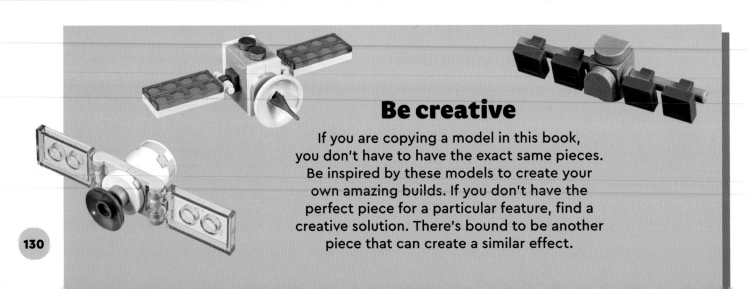

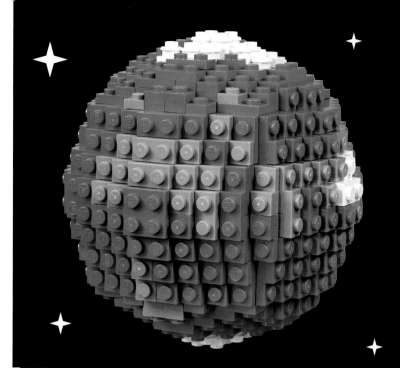

Which scale?

LEGO models can be built at any scale. Minifigure scale means a minifigure can sit or live inside your LEGO model. Microscale is anything smaller than minifigure scale. Lots of the models in this book are microscale because they are based on things that are huge in real life. Imagine building a LEGO Earth that was in minifigure scale!

THIS MODEL IS OUT OF THIS WORLD!

I COME IN PIECES!

Think sideways

Using pieces with studs on their sides allows you to build in more than one direction. You can create more advanced models using this technique, such as spherical planets. Sideways building also allows you to add details, for example, to attach wings or satellite panels to spacecraft or eyes to aliens.

Surprise yourself

Just because you've always used a piece in a certain way doesn't mean you can't use it in a completely different way. Play around with your LEGO bricks and pieces. Every single element can fit onto another in at least one way.

A clockwork key looks like complex tech on the side of the Hubble Telescope

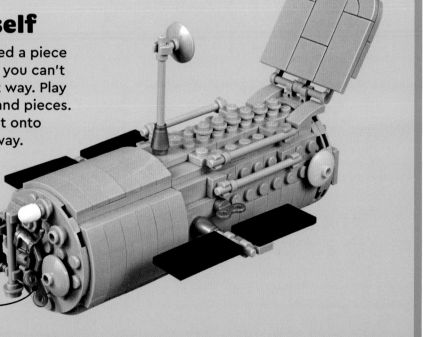

Useful bricks

LEGO® bricks and elements come in all kinds of shapes, sizes, and colors. It can be useful to learn more about your LEGO collection. As well as the main piece types you see below there are lots of interesting and unusual elements that can add detail to your LEGO models. You don't need all of these parts to make amazing LEGO models. Be creative with the pieces you do have!

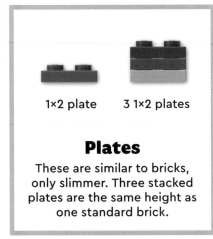

THE TINY BRICKS ARE MY FAVORITES!

⚠ Small parts and small balls can cause choking if swallowed. Not for children under 3 years.

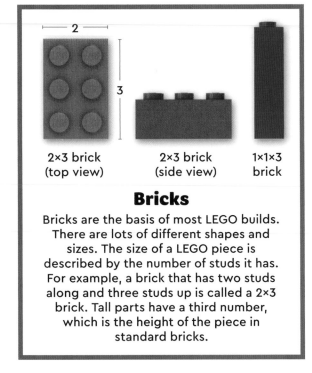

2×3 brick (top view) 2×3 brick (side view) 1×1×3 brick

Bricks

Bricks are the basis of most LEGO builds. There are lots of different shapes and sizes. The size of a LEGO piece is described by the number of studs it has. For example, a brick that has two studs along and three studs up is called a 2×3 brick. Tall parts have a third number, which is the height of the piece in standard bricks.

1×2 plate 3 1×2 plates

Plates

These are similar to bricks, only slimmer. Three stacked plates are the same height as one standard brick.

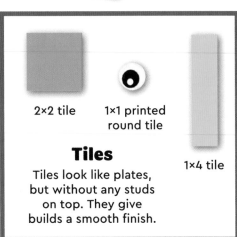

2×2 tile 1×1 printed round tile

1×4 tile

Tiles

Tiles look like plates, but without any studs on top. They give builds a smooth finish.

2×2 jumper plate

Jumper plates

These plates have just one stud in the middle, and allow you to "jump" the usual grid of LEGO studs. They are useful for centering things in your models.

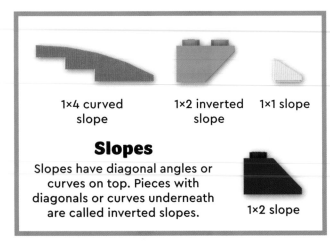

1×4 curved slope 1×2 inverted slope 1×1 slope

Slopes

Slopes have diagonal angles or curves on top. Pieces with diagonals or curves underneath are called inverted slopes.

1×2 slope

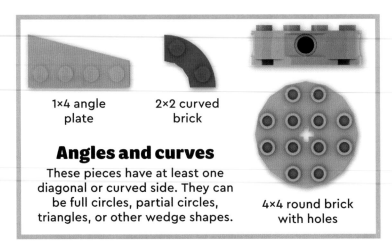

1×4 angle plate 2×2 curved brick

Angles and curves

These pieces have at least one diagonal or curved side. They can be full circles, partial circles, triangles, or other wedge shapes.

4×4 round brick with holes

Hinges

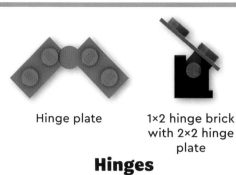

Hinge plate

1×2 hinge brick with 2×2 hinge plate

Hinge plates and hinge bricks can add motion to your builds. Using these allows models to move from side to side or to tilt up and down.

Side studs

Headlight brick

1×2 bracket plates

1×1 brick with four side studs

2×2×⅔ plate with side studs

1×2 brick with one side stud

Pieces with studs on more than one side allow you to build in multiple directions.

Special connectors

Not everything has to fit together with studs! Clips, bars, and friction joints can all add variety and movement to your builds.

Bar with angled stud

1×1 round plate with bar

1×1 plates with clip

Plate with ring of bars

Long bar with studs

1×1 tile with clip

Short bar with stopper

1×2 plate with bar

1×1 brick with clip

Plate with ball joint

Plate with socket

LEGO® Technic

These parts are used to make strong connections and mechanisms with robust moving parts.

LEGO Technic half pin

LEGO Technic pin

LEGO Technic 1×5 beam

LEGO Technic 1×2 brick with hole

LEGO Technic friction pin

LEGO Technic 1×2 brick with cross hole

LEGO Technic cylinder

LEGO Technic axle

Space specials

These pieces will come in handy for building spaceships, alien life-forms, and futuristic scientific equipment.

1×1 star

1×1 plate with tooth

Tail

2×2 radar dish

Mechanical claw

Robot arm

Skeleton arm

1×2 plate with turbine

1×1 round brick with fins

1×1 cone

Telescope

Cupcake

1×1 round plate with hole

Horn

4×4 radar dish

Meet the builders

The inspirational models in this book were created by a team of talented model designers who love to build with LEGO® bricks. We asked Tim and Simon some questions about their creative process.

Tim Goddard

What is your top LEGO building tip?
If you are re-creating a real object, look at lots of references, but don't worry too much about fitting in every detail. Think about the main things that are characteristic of what you are building and focus on those.

What was the most challenging model you built for the book?
The big black hole model (pages 82–83) was really tricky. The three-dimensional nature of the build combined with lots of colored semicircles is very difficult to make—but you can build anything with LEGO bricks!

Which of the models in this book is your favorite?
The large Milky Way mosaic (pages 88–89) is one of my favorites. It was challenging because of its size and detail and I have never built such a big mosaic before, but I was very happy with how it turned out.

If you were a minifigure, which of the builds in this book would you like to visit or try out?
Playing volleyball on the moon (pages 114–115) would be great fun! With low gravity, you can jump really high!

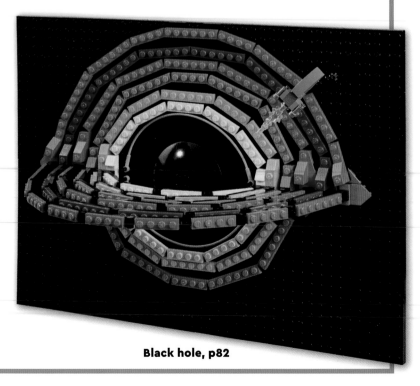

Black hole, p82

Simon Pickard

What is your top LEGO building tip?
Never compromise—there is always a solution to achieve the perfect look.

How do you plan your LEGO models?
I use research images to identify key features, which I then translate into LEGO form through trial and error.

What was the most challenging model you built for the book?
Getting all the angles right on the *Lucy* spacecraft (pages 98–99).

Lucy **spacecraft, p98**

If you could build anything in space with LEGO bricks, what would you build?
I would build more historical scenes of humanity's space exploration.

If you were a minifigure, which of the builds in this book would you like to visit or try out?
I would definitely want to drive the moon buggy (page 116)!

Moon buggy, p116

Glossary

artificial gravity
The creation of a force in a spacecraft that mimics gravity. This could be achieved by spinning the spacecraft.

asteroid
A chunk of rock smaller than a planet, which orbits the sun.

atmosphere
The layer of gases that surround a planet.

atom
A tiny piece of an element. Everything in the universe is made from atoms.

black hole
An area in space with incredibly strong gravity that means even light is pulled into it. Consequently, we can't see a black hole.

colony
A place established to create a habitat, a community, or a home for people to live in.

cosmonaut
A Russian astronaut.

dwarf planet
An object that is smaller than a planet like Earth but is big enough to have a round shape. Like a planet, it orbits the sun.

dwarf star
A small star that doesn't give off as much light as other stars. There are red dwarfs and yellow dwarfs.

ecosystem
Plants and animals that rely on each other and the environment they share.

element
A substance that cannot be broken down into simpler parts.

equator
The imaginary line that runs around the widest part of a planet.

galaxy
A group of billions of stars that, along with gas and dust, all move together in space. There are billions of galaxies.

gas
A material made up of atoms or small groups of atoms that are loosely scattered through space.

gaseous
Having the form of gas.

gravity
The force that pulls things together. Gravity makes Earth orbit the sun and the moon orbit Earth.

habitat
The environment where an animal lives.

hemisphere
One half of Earth. There is a Northern Hemisphere and a Southern Hemisphere.

hologram
A three-dimensional image made using laser beams.

impact crater
A hole on a planet made by a meteorite crashing into it.

inner solar system
The part of the solar system that includes everything up to and including the asteroid belt. Earth, Mercury, Venus, and Mars are in this.

light-year
The distance light travels in one year.

lobe
A rounded part of something that sticks out.

low Earth orbit (LEO)
An orbit area that is very close to Earth.

lunar plain
A flat area of the moon's surface formed when volcanoes erupted to fill a large impact crater.

mass
A measure of the amount of matter in an object.

matter
The stuff that things are made from.

meteorite
A rock that falls onto a planet or moon's surface.

meteor
A lump of rock or dust that burns up as it enters Earth's atmosphere.

microgravity
The reduced strength of gravity that objects experience in orbit, making them appear weightless.

molten
Describing something, such as rock, that has been heated to a very high temperature and is now a hot liquid.

moon
Any natural object that orbits around a planet.

NASA
The National Aeronautics and Space Administration (NASA) is a part of the US government that explores air and space. It was established in October 1958.

orbit
The path that one object makes around a more massive object in space. It happens because of gravity.

outer solar system
The part of the solar system that is beyond the asteroid belt. Jupiter, Saturn, Uranus, and Neptune are in the outer solar system.

radiation
Energy that moves in waves.

radio telescope
A large dish pointed at the sky that picks up radio waves to help scientists learn more about space.

radio wave
A type of radiation that is used in communication.

satellite
Any object that orbits around a planet. Moons are natural satellites but people have put many artificial ones into orbit around Earth.

solar panel
A device that absorbs energy from the sun, which is then converted into electricity.

solar system
The sun and everything that orbits around it.

speed of light
The fastest speed that anything in the universe can travel at—about 186,000 miles (300,000 km) per second. Only light and other types of radiation can move at this speed. No object with mass can reach it.

star system
A small number of stars that orbit around each other.

suborbital
A flight into space that does not complete an entire orbit around a planet.

supernova
A huge burst of light and radiation from a star that explodes at the end of its life.

terraform
To change a planet to be more like Earth so that humans can live there.

universe
Everything that exists, including all the planets, stars, and galaxies.

zero-G
Zero gravity, which is another way of referring to microgravity or weightlessness.

DID YOU THINK YOU'D HAD AN ALIEN ENCOUNTER?

Index

Senior Editors Laura Gilbert, Helen Murray
Project Art Editor Jenny Edwards
Designer Isabelle Merry
Production Editor Marc Staples
Senior Production Controller Louise Daly
Managing Editor Paula Regan
Managing Art Editor Jo Connor
Managing Director Mark Searle

Inspirational models built by
Simon Pickard and Tim Goddard
Additional models built by Jason Briscoe, Emily Corl, Nate Dias,
Jessica Farrell, Rod Gillies, Kevin Hall, and James McKeag

Photography by Gary Ombler
Jacket design by Jenny Edwards
Additional LEGO text by Simon Hugo
Space consultant Giles Sparrow

DK would like to thank:
Ashley Blais, Heidi K. Jensen, Martin Leighton Lindhart,
and Nina Koopmann at the LEGO Group. DK also thanks Megan Douglass
and Julia March for proofreading and indexing.

First American Edition, 2024
Published in the United States by DK Publishing
1745 Broadway, 20th Floor, New York, NY 10019

Page design copyright © 2024 Dorling Kindersley Limited
DK, a Division of Penguin Random House LLC
24 25 26 27 28 10 9 8 7 6 5 4 3 2 1
001–338905–May/2024

A catalog record for this book
is available from the Library of Congress.
ISBN 978-0-7440-9313-1

DK books are available at special discounts when purchased
in bulk for sales promotions, premiums, fund-raising, or educational use.
For details, contact: DK Publishing Special Markets,
1745 Broadway, 20th Floor, New York, NY 10019
SpecialSales@dk.com

Printed and bound in China

www.dk.com
www.LEGO.com

Your opinion matters

Please scan this QR code to give feedback to help us enhance your future experiences

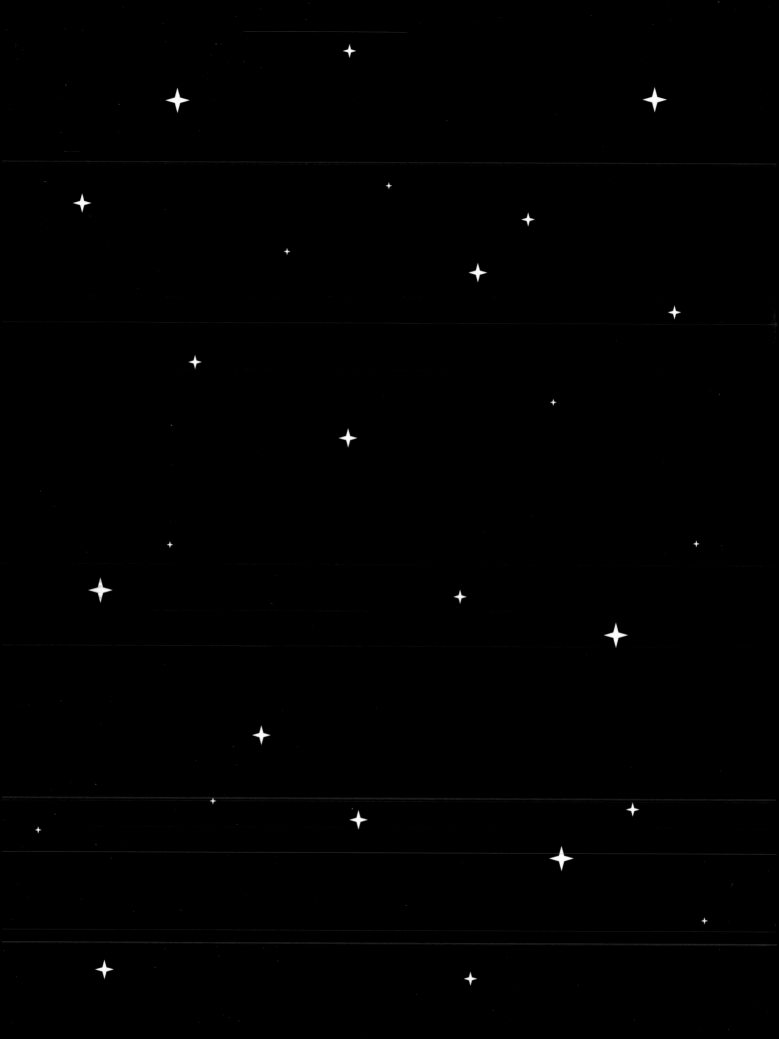